"WILL
I
ALWAYS
HAVE
ALZHEIMER'S?"

J. M. HORNER

ISBN: 978-1-326-55988-5

I dedicate this book to my loving family and friends and to all the people in the world with Alzheimer's and their carers.

ACKNOWLEDGEMENT

My profound and thoroughly deserved thanks to Mrs. E. Sutton for time spent converting my notes into immaculate typing and proofreading prior to printing.

CHAPTERS

LIFE

When I look, do I really see?

How does this fact affect me?

Do things happen beyond my gaze

Or do I see life in a kind of haze?

Is anything sharp and clear cut

Or is it because I am in a rut?

I search my mind to see things I have missed

But the Gods above, my eyes have kissed!

A cynic I would not like to be

But gullible, well, that is not me!

What is life and where does it lead?

With twists and turns it tends to deceive!

Do I keep a straight path making sure I focus

Or am I caught up in this hocus-pocus?

Where do I go from here, is it clear?

To keep tight hold of things that are dear

I have to make sure I am loved and secure

For these wonderful things I always want more

My blessings I count, I make sure of that

And for the Angels I put out a "Welcome" mat.

G. A. O'Hara
(2001)

PREFACE

1st October 2011

"A journey of 1,000 miles starts with the first step."

This old Chinese proverb, as well as referring to a long journey, could refer perhaps to anything which will take much time. The building of a suspension bridge, a skyscraper hotel, taking care of a very sick person, but here and now I refer to the writing of this book.

On 1st October 1979, I well recall walking on the beach at Abersoch in Wales. The weather was just like it is today - an Indian summer was giving us all high temperatures, blue skies and "wall-to-wall" sunshine. I wrote our names on the sand and added five or six large kisses. Sheer bliss!

My wife Dorothy and I were then both 41 years old. We could have passed for ten years younger at least. Holding hands, we turned heads with our obvious "joie de vivre" and glowing good health.

If only everyone's idyllic times could be "bottled" and fed back to us spoonful by spoonful. At least having experienced and shared these wonderful days, everything that life can bestow on us that is good and wholesome would be kept for the rest of our days in our memories.

Eighteen years ago, Dorothy was diagnosed with Alzheimer's disease. I shall hereafter, in this book, refer to this terrible affliction as Alzheimer's. Eighteen years in our case is almost a quarter of our lives. This time next year the ratio will be more than a quarter of seventy-four years.

I live my life strictly one day at a time. Why concern myself with tomorrow when today isn't over. I advocate this simple rule, as far as it is reasonably possible to follow, to all you Carers out there. The future is out of our control - it will not help us, the Carers, to stress ourselves beyond human endurance.

Many people have asked me what causes Alzheimer's. I was always led to believe that it was random bad luck. I do know that some people think it is a genetic illness but in Dorothy's case no one in her large family, parents or grandparents, has been a victim of this disease. This I do know for sure, that at the time of writing this book, there is no cure for Alzheimer's. There are various medications which slow down the remorseless progress of the illness. For several years, during the first and second stages, Dorothy took "Aricept" but this is useless in the third and final stage. In general though, in the majority of cases of Alzheimer's, the extension of stage two is quite lengthy.

It could take me a year to write this book. I hope not - it depends on the amount of time I can devote to it daily. However, I decided on the title years ago when I first considered writing a book, the main theme of which would be Alzheimer's.

Dorothy, who since her two strokes in 2006 and 2010, has been unable to speak a word, was, in the earlier years of Alzheimer's, a little "chatterbox". She would ask countless questions, sometimes with only a gap of seconds before asking the same question again, because she had forgotten she had asked and that I had answered her. So, the main question for years was: "Will I always have Alzheimer's?" I am not exaggerating in any way when I say that she could ask this question two, three, four hundred times a day. If only she could ask me now! Just once would do! My answer was always the same:"Yes, Dorothy, I'm afraid so but there are worse illnesses than Alzheimer's". People have asked me did I scream or shout the answer after the first hundred times and I can honestly say, that I never did.

You, dear reader, if you haven't already realised it, will come to know that a person with Alzheimer's will be unable to hold the answer to a question in his/her head for longer than a few seconds, or minutes, if the illness is only in its late first and middle stages. I have been blessed with infinite patience where

Alzheimer's is concerned. Learn to be patient, if patience is not one of your virtues then "learn patience".

A massive point I need to make in the preface of the only book I shall ever write is that I am hoping that the Alzheimer's Society will do all that is necessary to bring "Will I always have Alzheimer's?" (WIAHA) into print. If only one Carer in five buys a copy, the sales could top 100,000. I'm keeping my fingers crossed that the book will find its way on to W.H. Smiths bookshelves or even to the USA where there are countless millions of Alzheimer's carers. All royalties raised by the sale of WIAHA will go towards swelling the funds of the Alzheimer's Society. I don't wish for one penny for myself. My reward will be to see the book in print and to know that thousands of pounds will go to such a worthy cause!

INTRODUCTION

I was born on April 12th 1938 in an area of Manchester known as Withington. A few weeks later I was christened at the local church and was officially known thereafter as John Michael Horner. On May 28th 1938 a few miles towards the north side of Manchester, in a district called Newton Heath, my lovely wife was born and given the name Dorothy Pattison. We met on Monday, December 5th 1955, at Dorothy's place of work in Manchester's city office to audit the accounts. She was known as a Local Government Worker, her specific job being that of a shorthand typist. I was a junior audit clerk and Bill Barker and I had arrived at this Manchester Town Hall office to check a year's transactions.

A first date on December 12th 1955 led to engagement, marriage and the subsequent arrival of our four babies and the trials and tribulations with which all parents are faced. My grown-up children are aged 45, 48, 50 and 53. Looking back, I consider the best year ever was 1968, the children then being 2, 5, 7 and 10. Dorothy was a full-time mum and housewife. She resumed working part-time in 1972. My widowed Mum was inspirational for all six of us but she was to die in 1976, aged 63. Her loss was mind-numbing to the extreme.

Dad was a larger than life character. Everyone liked Norman. Of my parents' genes I was to receive the patience of my Mum and the steel of my Dad. I have a placid, cheerful nature; but I have the ability to look after myself in the event of anyone trying to take advantage, which invariably happens to us all as we journey through life.

Norman's life was to end in February 1964 at the early age of 57 from a virulent form of cancer. Forty seven years ago cancer was not as treatable as it is today.

Mollie, my Mum, lived her remaining twelve years enjoying her grandchildren and life in general. She loved coming to stay long weekends with us. Where have those delightful years gone? In an eighteen months period kidney failure was to claim her life in 1976. As with my parents' lives and Dorothy's, forever would not be long enough to have them in my life. I'm holding on to every day that I still have Dorothy but, eventually, grief will be the price I have to pay for love.

So, on to the chapters of WIAHA. They will contain a wide cross-section of Dorothy's journey through the three stages of Alzheimer's up to where she is right now, immobile and unable to speak a word, due to a massive stroke. She has been lying in bed for almost six years, longer than the duration of World War II.

Her life could perhaps now be measured in days, or weeks or months, but even in her deplorable state of health, I am not ready to let her go!

CHAPTER 1

"HELP THE CHIP PAN'S ON FIRE!!" (x2)

The title of my opening chapter, gives away any secrets of what the chapter may contain. A chip pan fire is a serious occurrence in anyone's home and after the first of two chip pan fires on consecutive Sundays, I was shocked that Dorothy had done something she had never done before in thirty-something years of being a housewife.

In the early 1990s, we often had a trip out somewhere on a Sunday afternoon and this particular Sunday was just like many sunny days of a better-than-average summer that year. We had been to Southport and parked on the beach, sat in the park, watched the bowling and window-shopped along fashionable Lord Street, then home to a classic, quick meal of two eggs on chips. Some cricket was on the television as I relaxed in my favourite armchair. I could hear activity from the direction of the kitchen and could visualise two lovely fried eggs on a mountainous helping of golden chips. My mouth was watering.

I think I must have dozed off for a few minutes. I awoke with a start, thinking that the shouting was coming from the television - perhaps an appeal for a run out or LBW. The shouting, however, I was quick to locate. Running into the kitchen I was met by a sight I had never seen before. The chip pan was well and truly on fire; flames were licking the kitchen ceiling and the heat was intense. In a split second I knew what was required - run the cold water tap, wet a tea towel and place it over the chip pan, cutting off the supply of oxygen to the fire, thus ending its brief and rapid upsurge.

I only had a second to act and running water and a wet tea towel seemed not to be the quickest way to save "Horner Towers", Instead, as the back door was already open, I gripped the chip pan handle and carrying the flaming object, placed it on the ground between the back of the garage and the front of the wood shed. Now seemed like a better time to place a wet tea towel over the still flaming chip pan. Seconds later the fire was extinguished and the golden brown chips had been reduced to blackened objects that even a stray, starving cat would not have wished to eat.

Dorothy, bless her, was mortified. I consoled her with a cup of tea and made us beans on toast whilst she relaxed in the lounge. It was a "one-off" as far as I was concerned but Dorothy even later that evening kept repeating, "How could I have set a chip pan on fire after all these years?"

The chip pan was not a "write off" by any means and the following day I restored it to near-perfect condition and on shopping day that week, Dorothy replenished the cooking fat. Sunday's mishap was a thing of the past and the Horner household was back to domestic bliss, or so I thought!

Sunday came along again, as Sundays always do. That day we decided to visit a local beauty spot known as Hollingworth Lake, just a short drive from home. We would have taken a flask of coffee with us, along with a snack. This enabled us to stay out longer before the hunger pangs kicked in. The planned two eggs on chips sounded even more appetising because we had missed out on them the previous Sunday.

I made a cup of my finest for us as Dorothy busied herself with the potato peeler. Off I trundled into the lounge to read the Sunday paper. What more could a man ask for on a Sunday evening? The smell of chips frying a few yards away. Dorothy really did make the best eggs on chips, this side of the Equator.

At first, I thought I was reliving a déjà vu scenario from the previous Sunday. Dorothy's almost hysterical scream from the kitchen seemed like an echo from the near past - last week. I think my legs were moving even before the message was sent down to them from my brain. Hurling myself forward I collided with my terrified wife who was running into the hall from the kitchen.

Automatic pilot takes over at a time like this. Dorothy, during the summer months, always cooked with the back door open: this saved a vital split second as I grabbed the chip pan handle and carried the burning, flaming pan to the exact sport as on the previous Sunday. I didn't pause to think about dousing a tea towel in water and extinguishing the flames in the kitchen. These flames were even more fierce but I'd had a "dummy run" the previous Sunday. I was an experienced "flaming-chip-pan extinguisher". As reported previously, the tea towel did its job and I returned to the kitchen to comfort my sobbing wife. My brain was being bombarded with an ever-increasing number of questions.

One fiery chip pan on a scale of 1 to 10 barely scored a one. It could happen to anyone who was a little preoccupied. Two "towering inferno" chip pans in seven days, was the "deafening silence" in my throbbing brain. On the scale of 1 to 10, this was a resounding 10!

That Sunday evening we talked and talked until past our usual bedtime. I knew that Dorothy must have some kind of a problem and I could see that she was scared. I hugged and kissed her and blamed what had happened on her hysterectomy operation but small things were now falling into place like a real life jigsaw puzzle.

Dorothy was an excellent cook and her baking skills were also of the highest order. For decades during the years our four children had lived at home, she had cooked countless wonderful hot meals - pies, puddings, tarts and buns - but within the last two or three weeks I had spotted the odd slight cooking errors - potatoes under- or over-cooked, mushy pasta, cremated toast, tepid cups of tea made with water which was way off boiling temperature. Scones not fully baked, jam tarts over-baked, etc.

My brain throbbed from constant thought. Dorothy looked quite well: a little drawn perhaps due to the previous year's hysterectomy operation. At 54 years old, she looked at least ten years younger. Years of keep fit, healthy eating and never having smoked and just the odd glass of red wine had worked marvellously in her favour.

I remembered two months previously waiting for her at 5.30 p.m. in the car and seeing her walk down the six or seven steps of the office block, with a frown on her face and without the usual bundle of letters, which we posted at the main Manchester sorting office. "Can't find the letters to post", she mumbled. I locked the car and proceeded to the second floor with my apologetic wife by my side. A quick search proved the mail was not in any of the offices. "Let's try the Ladies toilets" I suggested, which was, of course, where the neatly rubber-banded pile of letters had been left, on a small vanity unit.

Two or three weeks after the second chip pan fire I was on a rest day from my job. Dorothy started her job at 10.00 a.m .and I would drive her into Manchester city centre and drop her off outside her place of work. In the small shopping area close to "Horner Towers" is a chemist's shop. Dorothy asked me to stop so that she could purchase something. The shop was on the other side of the road. I saw her leaving the shop, heard her call "Bye" over her shoulder. I started the car's engine. Suddenly there was a squeal of brakes. I swivelled my head rapidly to the right just as a car missed hitting Dorothy by inches, the irate driver snarling "bloody idiot". She had run headlong, without looking, almost into the path of a car.

Oh my God! It was time for me to act and act quickly. On the way into Manchester I called at the Health Centre and we made an appointment for the following day. We were about to embark on a long, long journey.

I slept fitfully that night. Dorothy's breathing was regular and relaxed. On waking, she remembered that she had a doctor's appointment for 9.15 a.m. and I recall thinking that because we were such positive-thinking people that the day's appointment would go well.

CHAPTER 2

CT SCAN - WHAT EXACTLY IS ALZHEIMER'S?

I'd booked a double appointment the previous day to ensure adequate time for our questions. It was just as well. Dr. Mellor listened to our account of the events outlined in Chapter 1 and put the information into the computer. He gave Dorothy a brief general medical and then stated it was time for the "mini mental test". Little did I know how critical this short list of twenty questions was to prove. The questions were simple - the answers easy. However, Dorothy struggled with most of them, scoring a meagre six correctly. I realised that in my head I had answered all twenty correctly. The most difficult question was to spell the word WORLD backwards; the easiest, perhaps, in which county were we residing. A child of ten could and would have scored at least 15 or 16 out of 20.

Dr. Mellor then discussed the next phase to identify Dorothy's obvious problem. He gave us a letter of referral to enable a CT scan to take place the following day.

A CT scanner is an X-ray machine which can produce cross-sectional images of soft tissues. Its purpose is to find evidence of disease or malfunction in many areas of the human body - in Dorothy's case, her brain. The full title of a CT scanner is "Computerised Tomography Scanner". I thought Dorothy's CT scan results would be available to us in a couple of days or so. Ten days would have been closer. However, it was Dr. Mellor who conveyed the result by telephone. At 7.30 a.m. he told us that he started his surgery 30 minutes early so as to open his mail.

I remember that telephone call as plain as plain. He started the conversation with a completely ironical "I've good news for you and bad news, Mr. Horner". I replied that I'd prefer to hear the good news first. "Mrs. Horner hasn't got a brain tumour" said he, "but the bad news is that she has Alzheimer's disease". He gave me the titles of some books about Alzheimer's and said that a six-months sick note would be waiting for me at reception to collect on Dorothy's behalf.

I couldn't risk leaving Dorothy at home all day whilst at work. I was able to terminate my job on compassionate grounds reasonably easily. I've never been one to worry about the financial side of life but here we both were, a week ago earning salaries and now we were jobless and salary-less. My termination lump sum went towards paying off the mortgage and part exchanging the old family car for a brand new one which I knew would last us 10 years without massive repair bills. We would manage, we always had in the past, with four children and Dorothy a housewife. The future looked uncertain but our cup had always been half full, never half empty. Dorothy's first question to Dr. Mellor a couple of weeks later made me smile inside. For someone with early onset Alzheimer's, as the first stage of the illness is known, it was a pertinent question. "Will I die any sooner because I have Alzheimer's" she asked. The doctor paused for a few seconds before replying, "No Dorothy, you will live your life to its completion but from now on you'll always have Alzheimer's". It was a straight answer to a straight question.

My main question to Dr. Mellor, and please do bear in mind that Dorothy was in the very early stages of what is known as stage 1 (stages 2 and 3 quite obviously to follow), was what medication was available for her.

You will readily understand the two ensuing stages of Alzheimer's supersede each other in severity, There are no hard and fast rules to the speed at which Alzheimer's will progress. I have known of cases where the three stages have telescoped into three years and the patient has died from the effects of pneumonia. The American President, Ronald Reagan, lived for twenty something years with Alzheimer's and died well into his eighties.

Dr. Mellor mentioned the name of a drug called Aricept which very soon was to play a major part in our lives. A Consultant would decide if or when the patient was suitable to be considered for it. I advise all you carers out there to push determinedly so that your loved one will benefit from its use.

"Post code lottery" has been mentioned countless times as to whether Aricept will be prescribed or not. Budgets for many health areas cannot afford some higher priced medication but please push, push, push determinedly for it to be prescribed. You will be successful. In extreme circumstances Aricept can be bought over the counter at your local Chemist but it will cost you approximately £130 for 28 days supply.

When a consultant stopped Dorothy's repeat prescription because he thought it was no longer of any benefit I paid for four months supply because I still thought it was. After the four months a different consultant took over and put Dorothy back on it without me even asking him to do so. She remained on it for a further two-and-a-half years with all the resultant benefits.

Alzheimer's presently has no known cure! Maybe next year, or in five years or ten years time a fabulous drug will be unveiled to end this remorseless disease which blights millions of lives worldwide.

Once Alzheimer's has been diagnosed there is no going back. The brain cells affected will die and never grow back. Starting at the front of the brain the disease travels backwards. There is a similar disease to Alzheimer's known as Picks Disease. With Picks the brain cells are destroyed from the back of the brain to the front. The final outcome is the same as Alzheimer's.

Imagine the Empire State Building in New York at midnight with every light in every room on every floor lit up like a Christmas tree. Then imagine from the very top floor the light in every room are slowly turned off one by one, floor by floor down to the ground floor. That, dear reader, is how Alzheimer's destroys a brain. One light at a time, one brain cell at a time.

Many people confuse Alzheimer's with senile dementia, a condition many elderly people contract in later life. This is not Alzheimer's but appears to have similar symptoms. In old age we all become forgetful as the brain shows signs of wear and tear.

The youngest person I have personally encountered with Alzheimer's was Hilary, who was twenty-three. She was a student nurse when she was diagnosed with Alzheimer's via a CT scan. The last I heard of poor Hilary was that at the dreadfully young age of twenty-three she was institutionalised and being fed through her stomach by the PEG system. More about the PEG system of feeding and insertion of medication later in the book.

Alzheimer's has three distinct phases or stages. The patient passing away during stage three could do so because of a heart attack, a stroke, pneumonia or anything of a serious nature. As stated the three stages divide the illness into separate sections. Stage one would never be mistaken for stage two, nor stage two for stage three. You, as the carer, would witness one stage reaching its end as the next starts.

A stage reaching an end could take weeks or months before you notice more deadly symptoms revealing themselves. Death could occur in stage one or stage two as the result say of a stroke but generally it is during stage three. So, as we see, the patient will pass away with Alzheimer's but the cause of death would be a stroke.

In Dorothy's case, stage one lasted quite a long time - about three years. At the end of two years her consultant prescribed Aricept. The threshold of stage two would appear to be an ideal juncture at which to introduce this powerful medication. Its main purpose is to slow down the middle stage and extend it for as long as possible. This was to be a little short of seven years in Dorothy's case. Then, of course, the horrendous stage three takes over and Aricept is no longer of any benefit..

To begin with, in the area of Manchester - New Moston - where Dorothy and I live, neighbours would not accept that Dorothy had Alzheimer's and many said as much. Now towards the end of stage three most people just stay away, You, the carer, like me, will need to be inwardly strong to endure this situation. With the help of family and "real" friends, this is possible.

If I were asked to describe Alzheimer's in a few words this would be my reply: "Alzheimer's takes away the very soul of a person". We, the carers, have a tremendous responsibility. A victim of Alzheimer's can very often become lethal if left alone for too long. It has never been in my mind to place Dorothy in a care home or, as the years progress, a nursing home. Consequently, if you proceed along the same path as me, you will be storing thousands of minute pieces of care information in your head. This information you must share with the people around you - your family, friends and the people you will meet at say, Early Onset Dementia Centres.

I've lost count of the number of people who have said to me that if Dorothy really tried, she could start remembering again. One of the major symptoms in both the first and second stages is that I could question Dorothy concerning the occasion of our first meeting (in 1955) and she would be able to remember this but she would not be able to recall her evening meal by bedtime.

People in the first and middle stages of Alzheimer's may look perfectly normal but will lose their social skills one by one. By words or actions they will draw attention to themselves.

The title of this book as outlined in the Preface, was decided on when for several years Dorothy would ask "Will I always have Alzheimer's?" several hundred times each day. Yes! Several hundred times each and every day but one day the question stopped and she never, ever asked it again. Oh! that she were still asking it and speaking!

Two strokes within four years during the third stage have left Dorothy paralysed and mute - but more of that in another chapter.

So Alzheimer's gives the impression of the victim looking quite normal, with the inability to perform everyday, normal tasks and with a complete lack of short-term memory.

The future for you may look daunting dear carer but live your life one day at a time, don't worry about Wednesday if it is still Tuesday and you can, and will, prevail over this fearsome illness.

Again, I urge you, the carer, to press for Aricept to help your loved one to extend, as long as possible, the middle stage.

It was beneficial to Dorothy for several years. The second stage is not too bad and anything that delays the onset of the terrible third stage is worthwhile striving for.

CHAPTER 3

STAGE ONE: "HAS DOROTHY REALLY GOT ALZHEIMER'S?"

Waking up with Dorothy by my side in 1994 was mind-boggling in the extreme. She was in her mid-fifties but, as ever, looked ten years younger. How? Why? Prior to the experiences with the chip pan I did not see this coming. But there it was, dear Dorothy and I were starting off on the scariest journey of our lives. At least she had me to care for her.

I would attend to my bathroom ablutions, whilst Dorothy was still enjoying her sleep, and make us a cup of tea to drink in bed. We would chat during our "cuppa" and eventually make our way downstairs for breakfast, usually fruit, cereal and toast.

Because I had started to cook all the meals and make sure Dorothy was never in a position of danger, it was difficult for me to accept for months after her CT scan that she had been diagnosed with Alzheimer's. By now I knew about the three stages, the fact this illness was absolutely deadly in its progression and what was the prognosis? Two years, four years, ten years? I couldn't think about this for too long so I would try to occupy my mind with something else - anything but the "A" word.

In those far-off, early days, my caring duties were quite fundamental: cooking, cleaning, Dorothy's personal hygiene and the general supervision of someone who appears to look like an adult but needs the care and attention of a young child.

If I had a fiver for everyone who said "They've got it wrong, she definitely hasn't got Alzheimer's" during those early days, I would have quite a few hundred pounds. I even began to doubt it myself but Dorothy's CT scan was positive and Dr. Mellor had seen the X-ray.

For the first few months of becoming a Carer, I was still in the working mode. During the mornings I worked my way around the house decorating every room and finishing off by painting the outside. In the afternoon it was "our" time. We visited the coast, local places of interest or visited friends and relatives.

I was amazed at Dorothy's long term memory but appalled that things which were happening daily, could not be retained in her head even an hour later. Constantly day after day, week in, month out she would ask the same question, "Will I always have Alzheimer's?", between 200 and 400 times each day). "I'm afraid so but there are worse things than Alzheimer's!" I would reply.

People have said to me over the years "I bet it drove you insane" or, "Did you lose your temper with her every day?" The honest-to goodness answer is, Dorothy's single question didn't affect me in any way. I was always glad to answer her and years on, especially now she is completely mute, wish she was still asking it.

During stage 1, I became increasingly aware that people were beginning to avoid us. Dorothy's friends, friends and relatives and neighbours stopped their visits and stayed away. Neighbours didn't ask me how Dorothy was keeping and on one black day she called across to a woman living opposite to us who completely "blanked" her.

I have found over the years, right up to the present time, that poor Dorothy has been ostracised by local people but you, also, as a Carer of a sufferer of Alzheimer's, like me, will face ostracism.

Our family Doctor now is Dr. N. Morris. Not only is he an excellent Doctor but a thoroughly decent human being. Nothing is ever too much trouble. Without an appointment, I've actually seen him between patients on his schedule and he's promised to visit Dorothy after his last patient has been seen. You deserve all the praise you receive Dr. Morris, not only from me but from many others of your patients whom I know.

Local people at the Failsworth Health Centre, Manchester, are very fortunate because all the Doctors and nursing staff are of the highest calibre.

Dr. Morris once replied to my question regarding Dorothy and I being ostracised that this would not happen if Dorothy had cancer and not Alzheimer's. "People are afraid of anything to do with the brain" he stated. He went on to say that over 100 years ago people avoided a house where a cancer victim lived. Now the population accept cancer without any associated ostracism. Cancer thankfully can go into remission and, of course, modern treatments have an excellent success rate. Again I say, there is no cure for Alzheimer's. Only medication to slow down the middle stage.

My thoughts, reminiscences and reflections of Dorothy entering the sinister, lonely world of Alzheimer's in the mid-1990s are now, as then, a kaleidoscope of hopelessness, hope, fear, courage, lethargy, raised spirits, sadness, happiness, today, tomorrow and all the mental aberrations my brain can conjure up.

I'm a great believer in self help. Alzheimer's will never go away so we, the Carers, must learn to live alongside it. If we succumb to feelings of dread and despair our loved one will suffer directly and indirectly. We have to be at our best. I'm not telling you it's easy but it's manageable, with practice.

If you, the Carer, reading my story of how "we" handled Alzheimer's haven't a Social Worker, I suggest you telephone Social Services and enlist their help. Your allotted Social Worker will outline all the help available to you and your loved one. We really do need every last vestige of help of any description.

CHAPTER 4

SELF HELP

"Self help" is exactly that. I suppose you could call it by the old-fashioned terminology of "I can and I will". Either way, it is you, dear Carer, coping with Alzheimer's on the "front line" or at the "sharp end" of everything. You will need to be at your best every day or at the very least to give each day your "best shot".

I have, even before Alzheimer's, tried to make sense of life and death by searching into the "inner self" for patterns of order, cohesion, balance and "inner peace of mind".

You would have thought that after the horrors of World War One there would never have been another war. Wrong! Twenty-one years later World War Two was even more horrendous and since then, right up to the present moment, wars are fought and nothing is learned! Do we live in a society we deserve?

If ever a word was made-to-measure for an Alzheimer carer, it's the word "survivor." We have to survive so-called friends, neighbours and relatives not even making a telephone call or walking from next door, across the road or round the corner to ask about our loved one. We have to survive the slow disintegration of loved ones passing from normality to a hideous caricature of their former selves. We have to survive because there really is no alternative. Don't feel bitter, feel better!

Arguably, the most important virtue, we, the Carers, can possess, is the positive moral quality which will give us confidence. With confidence, which comes from within us all, lies an immense amount of power and love to create all that we will ever need in life! We must embrace life with a feeling of courage, trust, fulfilment and joy for the only life we will ever have.

Dorothy had two sayings she used for as long as I have known her, even up to the second stage of Alzheimer's; "This is not a dress rehearsal" (our lives) and, "You've got to rise above it" (troubles).

Within ourselves is "the higher self" and "the lower self". When our "higher self" is in charge, we are filled with joy, creativity, intuition, peace, power, love and all good, positive things. "The higher self" exudes confidence and all is right with the world. "The lower self" fills us with despair, self- doubt, fear, anger, helplessness, scarcity and all things negative. Your confidence drops and all seems wrong with the world. Treat "lower-self" mode just as a bad habit, which can be broken. Train yourself to be only a "higher-self person". Think of "higher self" as the high road. We really do not want to be trundling along on the low road with two punctured tyres. The "higher self" in us will demand the high road with picturesque views and a pleasant, easy journey.

If you keep repeating "I'll handle it", then this affirmation can give you an enormous sense of peace and tranquility when the frightening "What if" tries to take over. We really can handle whatever life throws at us if we listen to the voice of "I'll handle it" and kick the "What ifs" in the backside!

If a glass is half full, it is either half full or half empty. You and you alone can see the glass as half full. Half empty is negative (bad); half full is positive (good). Get into the good habit of seeing life in its best light; in full colour instead of the gloomy, black and white and grey of depression. Be a glass half full person!

Count your blessings. Even as a Carer of someone with Alzheimer's, there is much to enjoy still in life. If you pass a cemetery, ponder on the fact that the people buried there would love our problems. We have this one life for oh! such a limited period of time. We still have our loved one and stages one and two are endurable for both the Carer and the Alzheimer's patient. Lead from the front! So many people are relying on you! Try to be there not just as a Carer, but for your children, grandchildren and friends. It's not as difficult as you might think. You did not cause the Alzheimer's so no guilt is involved but it has, by fate, fallen on us to do our very, very best! Whatever cards are dealt us in life, however bad things may seem, we can choose how we react. No one can ever take away our reactions to experiences in life! Basically say "yes" to yourself when things appear to be going wrong. Too many times our first reaction is a bellowing "Oh, no"! This is negative. "Yes" will start off a positive flow of thought within your brain.

Although not immediately obvious, blessings can come from nowhere. Hence the time-honoured saying, "Out of bad comes something good". An example of this could be that as a Carer, I have spent much more time (quality time during the initial years) with my wife than I would have had if we had both been working.

Saying "yes" to life's challenges creates a deeper meaning and purpose to our lives. Be very proud of what you have achieved as a Carer! I am! You, as a Carer of your loved one automatically become a Very Special Person (VSP). People may ignore us, even ostracise us, but let them do their worst, we are VSPs!!

Learn to trust your instincts, your gut feelings. You will be surprised at the good advice your subconscious can give ..... When you listen. Remember as you learn, you cannot lose! Do not blame others if things go wrong. Blame is a powerless act. If you see all your decisions as "right decisions", it will be much easier to take responsibility for them. The big trick in life is not to worry about making a wrong decision, it is knowing how and when to correct it!

Keep a clear head. Try hard not to become confused and, ultimately, dispirited. Confusion will drive you "off course". Sit down and think, "How can I get out of this dead end I've backed into?" Positive thought will come riding into view very shortly. Yes!! Confidence is one of the greatest attributes anyone could have. Confidence is the positive thought that we can overturn any bad situation or traumatic experience. Think for the logical way out; there nearly always is one. Confidence in ourselves as a Carer will get us out of bed in the morning, ready to face possibly another daunting day. Confident people are like magnets. As your confidence grows, you draw people into your life. You will learn that you never need to feel alone! Try working at increasing your level of confidence . We are what we think! Never forget that. Think positively! Never say to yourself "I can't do that", say instead, "I can do this!" The motor within our brain will assist us and , "Hey presto!" you'll be on your way.

Remember that as a person and an individual that you really count and rate highly. Your presence makes a difference, especially because you're a Carer. Remember the song: "Always look on the bright side of life". Train yourself to look for the beauty and blessings that surround us every moment of every day, despite the fact that our loved one has Alzheimer's. Never expect anything in life, then you are never disappointed. This is freedom in the highest sense but when you do receive something, this is a blessing and a bonus. Positive, confident thinking is food for us, body, mind and soul.

Listen to the best of who you are, the voice that tells you that you are important and loving and have nothing to fear. You are a person who has so many wonderful things to offer. Believe me, I'm here to tell you, it is absolutely true!!

CHAPTER 5

THE CARISBROOKE EARLY ONSET ALZHEIMER'S CENTRE

Situated in Ardwick East Manchester, the Carisbrooke Centre is an oasis in the desert for early onset Alzheimer patients and their Carers.

As previously stated, avail yourself, dear Carer, of the services of a Social Worker. He/she can assist you in many ways: informing you of what you as a Carer and your loved one are entitled to, help with the completion of complex forms and the addresses of local centres, such as the one in the chapter heading and also the availability of respite centres.

Dorothy and I must have fallen through the net initially because for well over a year we were not allocated a Social Worker. When we were, I was told about carer's allowance, disability living allowance and a possible place, two or three days a week, at the Carisbrooke Centre.

The carers allowance back then was less than £39 a week but it is your entitlement so complete the form. I missed out on over a year of allowances just because I wasn't aware of them and/or no one informed me of this valuable help.

Dorothy absolutely enjoyed her few years attending Carisbrooke Alzheimer's Centre. The patients are only allowed to attend until their sixtieth birthday or if incontinence occurs before then.

I met some lovely people during Dorothy's years at Carisbrooke - not just the patients and the patients' Carers who would bring them along and collect them later, but also the staff, spread very thinly amongst the patients but very friendly and dedicated.

Once a month we Carers would attend a meeting and exchange views, ideas and problems we were experiencing. "A trouble shared is a troubled halved!" Sometimes an Alzheimer's expert would give us a lecture or show us informative videos. You, as a Carer, cannot learn too much about contracting this insidious disease, its progression through the stages and how, as a carer, you can even extend the life of your loved one.

It was on my very first monthly meeting at Carisbrooke that I met Jean and Dave, the parents of twenty-three years old Hilary. Hilary was institutionalised somewhere in the Bolton area. She was fed by the PEG method through her stomach because poor Hilary was unable to swallow. Medication is also delivered directly into the stomach by syringe. Nationwide and worldwide there have been known cases of Alzheimer's sufferers younger than twenty-three but Hilary was the youngest in Britain at that time in 1996.

Hilary was a student nurse when she was diagnosed with Alzheimer's. She was a keep- fit enthusiast. We cannot begin to imagine how Jean and Dave must have felt when they were told, just like the rest of us Carers, that there was no cure for Alzheimer's.

I knew that Dorothy, at fifty-four, was young to have this deadly illness but at twenty-three with her life, in the main, still waiting to be lived, our hearts went out to Hilary's parents, who were then in their mid-forties - so sad. So sad.

Dave told me what a neighbour of his had said a couple of weeks previously. It seemed that the neighbour, as Dave was gardening, asked him how Hilary was progressing (so far so good). Dave quickly explained the latest medical news of his daughter, in hospital permanently, fed by PEG, etc. The neighbour listened intently before asking, "Don't you think she'd be better off dead?" This was either callous or unthinking but Dave was in tears by the time he'd finished telling me the final part of his distressing story.

There were people at Carisbrooke with Alzheimer's from all walks of life - a solicitor, machine-operator, secretary, even a musician from the Halle Orchestra. Eric was an exceptional person but, of course, Alzheimer's seeks out its victims randomly. Eric was so unlucky! His wife, Helen, had been able to procure, after much chasing around, that saviour of the victims of Alzheimer's - "Aricept". Poor Eric was perhaps that one in a hundred who was allergic to this wonderful medication. He really did persevere for weeks but it made him feel dreadful and caused constant vomiting. Finally, a distressed Helen made the decision to stop the medication. Helen and Eric Fletcher, such a delightful couple.

It was, during Dorothy's time at Carisbrooke that a staff member asked if I had enduring Power of Attorney over Dorothy's finances. This is more commonly known as Power of Attorney which gives legal authority to act for another person.

The form could, at that time (1997), be purchased from H.M. Stationery Offices. Dorothy and I signed it and had this witnessed by a staff member. The entire form then must be sent off for official stamping. This cost £50 fifteen years ago. I've a feeling it's much dearer now but it really is a prerequisite for later when your loved ones cannot handle their own affairs. The Power of Attorney form needs to be signed by the signatory in good time before they are unable to write their signature.

Carisbrooke conjures up happy memories for me when Dorothy was in the early years of Alzheimer's.

CHAPTER 6

OUR WORLD TRIP: "SUCH AN INTERESTING PLACE, THIS PLANET OF OURS"

Dorothy and I had always enjoyed foreign travel. We'd visited several countries but our most ambitious trip had been to visit New Zealand in 1986, staying for a stop-over in Singapore on the outward journey and Los Angeles on the return leg.

Even during the first year of Dorothy's Alzheimer's, I knew she would not always be "compos mentis" and so decided to travel as much as possible in the early years.

Late in 1994 we got our heads together and decided on which of over two hundred countries in the world we would include in our "one-off" world trip.

We had friends in South Africa and relatives in New Zealand. To these two countries we added: Malaysia (Kuala Lumpur), Japan (Tokyo), China (Beijing), Hong Kong, Australia (Sydney), Argentina (Buenos Aires), and Brazil (Rio de Janeiro) - nine countries in total, spread over a period of eight weeks.

Jean and Tony Ivell at "Pole Travel" in Failsworth, Manchester, helped us enormously with bookings and flights, etc. It is a family-run firm that puts massive companies to shame.

A week before we were due to fly out on 1st February 1995, Dorothy put a travel bag through the washing machine and obviously saturated the passports in one of the pockets. I dried them out but wasn't happy about their appearance. It was a good job that I checked this out with Jean and Tony. Their verdict was that the passports would not have been acceptable at Passport Control. They had passport application forms on the premises which Dorothy and I duly completed. Tony then said that we had insufficient time for postal application and that he would drive to

Liverpool Passport Office and purchase new passports for us and would also purchase for us the nine currencies we required and some American one dollar notes for tipping - always acceptable in any country.

Two days before flying off to South Africa I collected all the flight tickets, including domestic flights, which Jean had stapled together in flight/date order. What a lovely couple! Nothing was too much trouble.

I well recall arriving for our "shuttle" flight from Manchester Airport to Heathrow, Terminal 4. Our flight tickets, all "concertinaed" together and about two inches thick caught the immediate attention of our check-in official. "Where the heck are you two off to?" she gasped.

We were independent travellers during the world trip. Our accommodation was all pre-booked except in New Zealand, where we were staying with relatives around Wellington before arriving in Aukland. "Easy peasy" to find a decent-looking hotel in a big city. Independent travellers are not met at the flight destination but taxis or coaches are plentiful. Day trips or half-day trips can be booked at the hotels by the concierge at reception. You are then picked up at the hotel. These day trips are magnificent, take my word for it.

Friends did await our arrival in Johannesburg. Doreen and Brian Perry met us at Jan Smuts Airport. After leaving freezing conditions in England on the previous day, within an hour of arriving at the Perry's lovely bungalow, Dorothy and I were swimming in their massive outdoor pool - absolutely delightful!

Many people have asked me, "What was your best day during the eight weeks?" So much to choose from but I would say, after much reflection , that day in China walking along the "Great Wall" and visiting the "Forbidden City", etc.

Each day gave Dorothy and I extreme pleasure. The sights and scenery, the smells and the noises of many different cultures are memories of which I have instant recall. Dorothy talked about the world trip for up to a year afterwards but then her memories faded. A myriad experiences were telescoped into eight weeks. Dorothy now no longer knows she even went but I'll never forget!

During our stay in Hong Kong, we had a chance meeting with a young Chinese man called Tony Ng. He was twenty two and the assistant manager of a small hotel, in a less fashionable part of Hong Kong. He spoke excellent English - the exception to the rule in Hong Kong. After an hour spent in his delightful company, he informed us that his day off was Sunday and if we would wish to, he would take us on a grand tour of Hong Kong.

He arrived at the "South Pacific", Room 917, at 8.55 a.m. Dorothy and I thought that we'd already seen most of this vast city but Tony proved otherwise. We went "everywhere": on buses, trams, ferries, trains and the vehicular railway up Victoria Mountain. We stood on the spot where Jennifer Jones and William Holden spoke their lovely lines in the film, "Love is a Many Splendoured Thing", filmed in 1955. The view is quite breathtaking! The three of us stood in wonder at how "all that" fitted into such a small area.

At 10.00 p.m. Tony took us to his favourite eatery. Well off the beaten track where tourists never venture, we enjoyed a seventeen-course meal of the best Chinese food Dorothy and I had ever tasted!

Back at Room 917, just before midnight, two very tired but "happy bunnies"! "What a day! What a captivating island!"

We kept in touch with Tony Ng for three or four years. He took up a new job in mainland China and eventually the letters stopped.

I could write a short book about our world trip. Suffice it to say, it was a wonderful experience for us. Dorothy enjoyed it hugely. All the flights took off on schedule and arrived on time.

Dorothy did this quite ambitious trip in her first stage of Alzheimer's. We were to travel for three more years before flying was no longer possible; more about that later in the book.

You, dear Carer, must make the most of the early years. If you don't wish to travel abroad, take regular holidays in this lovely island. The memories will always stay with you.

CHAPTER 7

"WHO IS THAT LITTLE GIRL?"

Sounds like a strange title for a chapter of a book but I suppose not if the book is about an Alzheimer's sufferer.

My grandchildren live in London, as, of course, do my two daughters and their husbands.

During this period of Dorothy's Alzheimer's, we would visit London as frequently as once a month and my daughters, not at the same time, would visit us at "Horner Towers". Dorothy idolised her grandchildren and she would generate much excitement in the days prior to a visit here. She would ask, in between asking "Will I Always Have Alzheimer's?", "Who's coming to stay here tomorrow?" Anything coming soon was always "tomorrow".

Eventually "tomorrow" would arrive and we went to meet the London train at Piccadilly Station. What excitement for us all! Dorothy could hardly wait to get home so that she could cuddle Jakson and Saffron. We would all play kiddies games and large quantities of Ribena and Jaffa Cakes were consumed.

The following day sticks in my memory. Saffron was just two (she is now twelve). After breakfast Dee, my daughter, took her two children round the corner to visit a family friend. They were gone for a little over an hour. Dorothy and I had been sitting in the lounge enjoying our morning coffee. The front door bell sounded and I let in my daughter and grandchildren. Dee sat next to Dorothy and me on the settee, the children spilling over onto the carpet to play with the new toys which I had recently purchased for their visit. "What a lovely scene" I remarked to Dee. "Enjoy them Mum and Dad" she replied, "they grow up so quickly, as you know". I nodded in agreement as Saffron got to her feet and climbed onto an easy chair. Dorothy, after a few seconds, looked at Saffron and said, "Who is that little girl?" Dee and I looked at each other: no words were said, the look in our eyes said it all. In just over an hour, Dorothy had forgotten who little Saffron was! I quickly explained to her that she'd forgotten, just briefly, because Saffron had left the house for an hour or so. I knew in my heart of hearts that the Alzheimer's spring had just tightened a tiny notch more. This was nothing, I knew, compared to what I could expect and experience in the future.

"Glass half full" syndrome must always, as a Carer, be at the forefront of what is possibly the most "hands-on" caring duties of any illness in the world. Don't even allow negative thoughts to take over; we, as Carers, are on the slippery slope.

CHAPTER 8

"EDDIE STOBART" - IT'S A WONDERFUL GAME

Dorothy and I have been travelling down to London since 1987 - that was the year that our elder daughter, Liz, moved to "the smoke". At the peak of our visits down south to London, we went as many as 12 or 13 times a year. These were the years following Dorothy's CT scan which confirmed her having Alzheimer's. By this time, our other daughter, Dee, was living and working in London.

For the last six years since Dorothy's first stroke, she has been unable to travel and I make the journey alone prior to Christmas and the birthdays of my grandchildren, Jakson and Saffron, which fall respectively on the 4th and 6th of December. I would not recommend completing the round trip in the same day but when needs must, as in my case, it has to be done. Setting off at 6.00 a.m. on a day with decent weather, few road works and no mechanical failures, I can arrive at Dee's house by 10.00 a.m. The return journey is normally a 4.00 p.m. start, arriving back in Manchester by 8.15 p.m. (ish) The total number of miles is 480.

At the beginning of Dorothy's Alzheimer's we played "I Spy" during the car journeys. The trouble with "I Spy" is that one can only use objects within the car, as the motorway changes by the second. Not the best game for a long trip. However, help was on the way in the shape of "Eddie Stobart's" massive green lorries - a game of "I Spy" just counting how many of "Eddie Stobart's" vehicles we saw on either side of the motorway. The game restarted on the return leg. Dorothy loved this new game and we continued it for years. In the latter years any green vehicle was deemed to be an "Eddie Stobart". Our record count was twenty-seven on a mid-week journey back to Manchester.

Even though I'm alone now on my yearly excursion to London, or any trip along the motorway, I still automatically count the never-ending number of "Eddie Stobart" trucks.

Yes, counting "Eddie Stobart's" is a wonderful game.

CHAPTER 9

"IT'S A, IT'S A, IT'S A TWOER!"

Any ideas as to what a "twoer" is?

It's what a young boy, about six years old called our tandem. Tandem was not yet in his vocabulary but this youngster was very impressed as we rode into view. We were on a holiday, Dorothy and I, in sunny Portugal, when we decided to hire out a tandem. It was very heavy, not too old and had three gears - only two were working but I quickly got the low gear operating and off we rode into the "wide-blue-yonder". Practising on the promenade, we didn't cause the slightest sensation amongst the holiday makers in Villamora. Neither of us had ever ridden a tandem before but we both very quickly grasped the golden rule; don't fall off!

In 1984, ten years before Dorothy contracted Alzheimer's, we loved every golden moment on this "bicycle-made-for-two". We even extended the period from three days to eight days, much to the surprise of the bicycle hire proprietor. He explained that most couples returned a tandem on the second day, even if they had paid for three days.

Gaining experience daily and becoming more adventurous, we rode further and further along the coastline. On day five or six of our tandem riding an incident occurred. I think accidents happen in foreign parts because holiday makers become too relaxed and throw caution to the winds. Dorothy and I didn't have a mishap on our tandem, fifteen miles down the coast from Villamora, but we could so easily have done. The brakes on this "dreadnought" of a tandem were not good - a five out of ten mark only. All right on the flat but here we were charging down this hill with the brakes on full. A "white-knuckle ride" in the extreme.

I could hear Dorothy whooping with delight but my mind was on how soon this downward dash would end and we would start

39

going up the other side. The answer to that was just seconds away. We shot into a wide clearing where the road ended, indicated by a low dry-stone wall, overlooking a drop into the Atlantic Ocean. A large hotel was on the left. Quick as a flash I weighed up my options: only two as it worked out. The wall was not an option; we would have arrived at the "scene of the accident". The second option was much better - a wide gap in the wall led to the hotel car park. We'd "scrubbed off" just sufficient speed to negotiate the turn into the open expanse of car park. Round and round we went until the tandem answered to the brakes and I heard Dorothy yell "Wow, that was fantastic!" We finished up quite close to a young couple sitting in their car eating ice cream cornets. I have never seen anyone, before or since, so open-mouthed in astonishment.

I didn't inform Dorothy about how "it really was" until we'd been back home a few days. She admitted that she'd had no idea and I explained, "That's how 'dead-end' got the name".

Two years later in Zakinthos (Zante), a delightful Greek island, we again hired a tandem for a few days . We cycled to a resort at the far end of the island, spending several hours swimming, sunbathing and enjoying a Greek meal. We had left the tandem in the shade but the extraordinary mid-afternoon temperature had caused the front tyre to explode.

Eighteen miles back to our hotel and to be quite honest, I didn't even have a Plan A, let alone a Plan B. No bike shops to be seen; no other cycles in sight. I don't know why Dorothy and I started pushing the tandem back. Eighteen miles at two miles an hour equals nine hours! Mission almost impossible!" We had been pushing for about an hour and were almost falling down with exhaustion because of the temperature. An idea came into my head about a story I had once heard of a cyclist having had a puncture, stuffed the tyre with grass and proceeded home; quite slowly, I was thinking.

Just then, the equivalent of a Manchester "white-van-man" came into view, travelling in our direction. I stood in the centre of the road and waved him down. What a lovely, warm-hearted Greek he was. I showed him the burst tyre, he didn't speak any English and we could only say "please, thank you, hello and goodbye" in Greek. He pointed to the rear of his vehicle and together we deposited the tandem into the ample space. He dropped us off outside the bicycle hire, we thanked him in Greek and I offered him some drachmas towards his petrol. Our new-found, Greek friend declined to accept our money but I half pushed it into the passenger seat where he would surely find it. What a day!

For Dorothy's forty-ninth birthday I bought her a "made-to-measure" lightweight tandem. I didn't want to wait the extra year until she was fifty. Dorothy turns seventy-four tomorrow, so, obviously, I collected the finished tandem twenty-five years ago tomorrow. This superb machine was Dorothy's pride and joy. It was built exactly to our correct size; a gent's frame front and a lady's frame back. I was the "Skipper" and she the "Stoker". Oh, how she enjoyed our excursions out and about.

Dorothy rode her tandem well into the first stage of Alzheimer's. However, one day I realised she had lost the knack of the basic tandem riding technique and we never ever rode it again - too dangerous.

After Dorothy had her first stroke and she became bedridden, the owner of a cycle shop just a mile away, name of Neil Orrell, converted the tandem into a solo bicycle. I well recall riding "Dorothy's tandem" to his shop for its conversion. The journey is approximately one mile but I did not enjoy that ride. I'd never ridden it by myself until that day. As I rode ever closer to Neil's shop I was thinking of the hundreds of rides and the hours of sheer bliss this machine had brought to me and Dorothy: the end of an era! I looked at our beloved tandem after delivering it to Neil's. I'd never see it again but I knew the solo bike would look fantastic. What an excellent job he made of it! Thanks Neil!

I have a friend called Tec, whom I have known since we started infant school together.

He calls to visit us quite frequently and eats a meal of fish and chips, homemade of course. If it's a decent day weather-wise, Tec brings his bike and we'll have a short spin out.

My bike is half a tandem. If it could talk it would be saying, "Where's Dorothy, that lovely 'Stoker?'"

CHAPTER 10

LOST IN LONDON E4

Not all the chapters in my book are in chronological order. Some may jump around because I'm not 100% sure when the chapter content occurred. I haven't kept a diary over the last nineteen years but my memory is still quite sharp. However, "Lost in London E4" is as clear to me as when it happened in September 1996.

Dorothy was in her third year of Alzheimer's. Lots of neighbours still thought I was making the whole thing up; mmm. We had been on our world trip the previous year in 1995 and Dorothy was still talking about it but only occasionally. Our first grandchild Alex had been born on 31st March 1994 and he had bonded well with his grandparents. He loved going walks, especially when we took him to Lloyd Park or the closer Highams Park. My daughter, Liz, had only moved to the Highams Park district of London from Walthamstow in April 1996. Not many people outside London have heard of this lovely suburban area. It takes its name from the nature park, complete with a lake, just down the road from Liz's house.

On· "this" evening in September 1996, Liz and her husband were taking in a show in the West End. I was in charge of their home, plus, of course, Dorothy and Alex. Dee, my younger daughter, had visited for her tea and was about to leave, time a little after 7.00 p.m., to travel the short distance by train to her flat in Walthamstow.

I suggested to Dorothy that she should walk with Dee and Alex down to the main road, about 300 yards right, along Handsworth Avenue, as far as the T-junction - a 100% straight line walk there and back. Dorothy said "I know, I know, you don't have to come with us". She'd walked along Handsworth

43

Avenue several times in the past few days and Dee said that she would turn them round at the T-junction. Dee even shouted, "Watch for Dad's car and that's outside Liz's house". Dorothy waved in acknowledgement and proceeded back along Handsworth Avenue.

Back at Liz's house, I think it was around 7.25 p.m., that I started to feel uneasy. I stood by the front garden gate and looked down the road towards the distant T-junction. Dorothy and young Alex were nowhere in sight and inwardly I cursed myself for not walking with them. "Fool, fool, bloody fool" I berated myself out loud, as I jogged down to the T-junction. Not there! I realised I felt anything but calm. I tried deep breathing but I had a deep, bad feeling in the pit of my stomach.

I jogged back to Liz's house by the circular route, in case somehow Dorothy had become lost and was still close to home. No sign of them. I even checked the platforms at the Highams Park railway station, then on to a children's play area, in a small park that we had all visited the day before. No sign of them! I asked people I passed if they'd seen a blonde lady with a toddler - none of them had.

Jumping into my car I criss-crossed the whole Highams Park area and surrounding roads for the next half hour. Nothing. It was rapidly becoming dark and I decided to ring 999.

A friendly lady took the particulars and said to ring back when the people who were "missing" had been "missing" for 24 hours. This, she told me, was police policy for "missing persons". I asked to speak to a more senior person and she passed me over to a Police Sergeant who then told me his Inspector would call me back in two or three minutes.

The Inspector stated that he had an aunt with Alzheimer's and, therefore, knew of the seriousness of the illness and of the possible danger my wife and grandson could be in. He said that he was giving the incident "A" priority and within an hour twenty police cars would be combing the area. Time seemed to stand still. The minutes slowly measuring the next hour, police cars constantly coming and going in case Dorothy had made her own way back. I kept telling them this would not be possible with an Alzheimer's sufferer. The Inspector, a worthy man, rang me several times to offer encouragement and to say that, "it was just a matter of time".

After a silence of about twenty minutes, suddenly the telephone rang. It was Liz enquiring if all was well within her household. She, of course, knew nothing of the drama that was unfolding. I lied to her before I even realised what I was saying. "Yes, Liz, everything's fine here, Alex is in his cot fast asleep".

Weeks after this terrible experience, Liz said that just a slight tone of my voice indicated that something was not right. I, of course, could not tell her at the time exactly what was happening.

Police cars were coming and going. Another one arrived and a WPC wanted a full description of Dorothy and Alex. I was almost losing my grip on reality as I informed her of the height, hair colour and the clothes they were wearing. Wake up, a voice was telling me from within my brain, this nightmare has gone on long enough! But I didn't wake up, this was harsh, cold reality, without the luxury of waking and thinking, "Thank God, it's only a dream!"

I was just thinking how I was going to explain to Liz and Francis when I became aware that a Vauxhall Astra had drawn up behind the police car with the two officers sending out the descriptions of Dorothy and Alex to colleagues who were out searching. A fair-haired lady in her thirties left her car and opened the rear passenger door. She helped Dorothy out followed by Alex. I was hugging my lovely wife and grandson before this fair-haired lady had even slammed the car door shut. Oh, what joy!!!

The lady's name was Debbie and she had thought that 10.20 p.m. was late for a middle-aged lady and a toddler to be out and without outdoor clothing. She had pulled up alongside Dorothy and asked if everything was alright. Dorothy had replied that she thought she was lost and that she had Alzheimer's. Dorothy couldn't remember where she was staying but said there was a big school on the other side of the road to where her daughter lived. Debbie took Dorothy to two schools but neither was "Highams Park High School". The third school was the correct one and on the left side of Handsworth Avenue she noticed a police car and parked behind it.

My gratitude to Debbie knew no bounds but I didn't ask for her telephone number or address. All I had was her Christian name and that she drove a silver Vauxhall Astra. My daughter was unable to thank her but Debbie, I'm sure, was the kind of person who was happy to have been a good citizen and helped two people in distress.

I gave Alex a quick bath and he was asleep before his head hit the pillow. Five minutes later, at just before 11.00 p.m., the front door opened and I explained to an astonished couple what had happened since they had left the house at 6.30p.m.

It was well into the small hours before I finally dropped off. My body was full of adrenalin and my mind too active. I'd got away with it last night. A wonderful person called Debbie had taken the time to help my wife and grandson. I knew that instead of Debbie it could have been a paedophile cruising around and inviting Dorothy into his car.

As Dorothy's Carer, I took full responsibility for what happened that evening. Dorothy's Alzheimer's had moved on "two more notches" during the day and I had made a massive mistake, in complete innocence obviously, but the "buck stops" with me.

At all times, in the first months of Alzheimer's or into the third stage, always expect the unexpected.

Ever since the sad abduction of Madeleine McCann in Portugal in May 2007, I have wondered would it be possible to place an electronic chip under the skin somewhere on toddlers and even older children? Placed in a stud earring or ring this would safeguard the child easily.

Pets have had the advantage of "chipping" or "tagging" for years now. Why not our most precious loved ones?

CHAPTER 11

ANGLESEY, GREAT FOR TANDEM RIDES

If, dear reader, you have never visited Anglesey, that wonderful island situated opposite the city of Bangor, North Wales, then rectify that omission as soon as possible. You won't be sorry.

The island of Anglesey covers an area of a mere 276 square miles. If it were a square, it would measure 16.5 x 16.5 miles. Consequently, no matter where you want to live on Anglesey, you are always within eight miles from the sea.

Anglesey, compared to many other areas of Wales, is comparatively flat but riding a tandem requires a strong set of calf and thigh muscles! The roads are definitely undulating. An important feature to bear in mind, if you are about to book a fortnight in Wales, is that Anglesey has the lowest rainfall, and the mildest climate, of any other area of this delightful country.

Puffin Island and Llanddwyn Island are bird sanctuaries and are the haunt of many species of birds, including the famous stormy petrel. The coastal scenery is staggering in places. Red Wharf Bay, Rhosneigr Bay, Malltraeth Bay and South Stack are just a few of the many places worthy of a visit.

The village of Newborough is the start of one of the best walks (or tandem rides) on Anglesey. At the crossroads in the village centre, head down towards the sea and Llanddwyn Island, with its lighthouse. Leaving the village behind, you will pass an ancient church on the right and as the road progresses downwards, for £3.- the car barrier will lift and you and your car are able to park all day, a mile further on. On our tandem each turn of the wheels rewarded us with fabulous views of the massive forests on either side of the road. Mostly freewheeling, we were always sorry when the road ended.

Forty years ago, Newborough beach was the best on the island, but now it's a little pebbly. It is still brilliant though. Many are the delightful days we've spent on the beach there, sunbathing and swimming.

Our favourite place on all of Anglesey was a 350 years old cottage just outside Malltraeth. We've stayed at "our cottage", as we used to call it since the early 1980s. Its name is "Bron Afon".

The first occasion we stayed at this quaint little cottage was during the month of September. We found the key under the plant pot by the front door and let ourselves in. A blazing fire was in the fireplace, sending up leaping flames. Stan Glover, the next-door-neighbour, had anticipated a cool evening. He had gone to the trouble of lighting a coal fire for Dorothy and me.

The following morning we called round to the cottage next door to introduce ourselves. What an absolutely lovely man Stan was. He was the caretaker or janitor for "Bron Afon", which was owned by his brother. Visitors to "Bron Afon" were expected to vacate the cottage by noon. New arrivals could only start to unpack their cases after 3.00 p.m. During the three hours before the new arrivals, Stan would clean the cottage and bring it up to the required standard of cleanliness, if that were necessary.

Over a coffee and Jaffa cakes, Stan, Dorothy and I got to know each other really well. He was a "Brummie". I've a feeling he was born on Anglesey and had moved to Birmingham in the 1930s but my memory is a little vague on that matter. Stan had this lovely Brummie accent which Dorothy couldn't understand. I got to know all the British accents during my National Service days, so I could "interpret" for her. These were the days before Alzheimer's and our tandem was leaning against a wall, ready for Dorothy and I to go exploring on it. Stan was suitably impressed and could hardly believe how light it was.

We talked for so long, that Stan stayed for the mid-day meal. He just fitted in so well. In the afternoon Stan took Dorothy and I on a tour of Anglesey. All the "off-the-beaten-track" places of interest that he and his lady friend had discovered down the years.

Stan's lady friend was a Doctor. Dorothy and I addressed her as "Doctor Mary" She was a lovely person and had a practice on the island. Stan was retired the year we found our lovely holiday retreat. In later years when Dorothy had started with Alzheimer's and we didn't need to return back to Manchester to our jobs, Stan allowed us to stay free, if no one was booked in for the following week. All we needed to pay for was the electricity. Happy days, in so many ways, in spite of Alzheimer's!

Judy, Stan's sister, started to live at Stan's cottage during the 1990s. She was a lovely lady and was also a "Brummie". She had worked for over forty years for Cadburys. That's a lot of chocolate she must have eaten.

Recently, I found an old photograph. I had taken it outside "Bron Afon". There were six people on it, all smiling their heads off: Stan, Doctor Mary, Judy, Ernie and his wife (Stan's friends) and Dorothy. On that day around 1991 when I took this photograph, all six were in reasonable to good health but one by one they passed away and only Dorothy is still around, albeit in what many people would describe as a state of health not worth being alive. We, that is myself and family, true friends, Doctor Morris and decent, good neighbours, believe her life is as sacrosanct as anyone else's. Dear readers, we need to extract every last ounce of living from our lives now and everyday!

One day, at our hideaway cottage, we had invited Judy and Stan for a cooked meal. Dorothy had not then been diagnosed with Alzheimer's, nor was she showing any signs of what was yet, more than 12 months away. I was entertaining our guests with home brew beer, white wine and chit chat. Dorothy was in the kitchen, cooking a roast and its "etceteras". Stan shouted a couple of times, "Lovely smell wafting from the kitchen, Chef!" Dorothy would walk into the tiny lounge, face beaming. She was an excellent cook, and, like all ladies, enjoyed being complimented on the fact. A shout from Dorothy informed us that dinner was served and we were to make our way into the kitchen/diner.

Dorothy must have cooked this meal a thousand times before. The beef was there in plentiful slices, lots of carrots and cabbage, but no Yorkshire pudding, no roast potatoes around the beef and only two new potatoes, per person, per plate. I'd bought a big bagful of potatoes from a local farmer only that morning. I looked at the plates and asked Dorothy, "Why have you only boiled eight new potatoes, Sweetheart?" Dorothy just mumbled that there looked to be lots and lots in the saucepan. I didn't mention the lack of Yorkshire pudding or roast potatoes. I'm sure Stan must have still been hungry after the main course. He loved new potatoes and must have remembered previous appetising meals with everything included.

Worse was to follow. Dorothy had made a large apple pie at home a few days previously. I remember it being placed in the fridge on arrival. Where was it now? We finished up opening a tin of peaches, which we ate with Vienetta ice cream. I found the apple pie the following morning in the wheelie bin, together with kitchen waste. Little did I know, this was the first step along a long, dark road, with no going back!

A few years later, Dorothy and I attended Stan's funeral. My lovely wife was well into the second stage of Alzheimer's by then. Judy passed away two years later. Thank you for a lovely friendship!

The very last occasion we visited "Bron Afon", Dorothy had a two-and-a-half hour rest from asking, "Will I always have Alzeheimer's?" Instead, every thirty seconds she asked me, "Where is it we're going to?" Little did I realise as I answered her question with, "We're going to Anglesey, Sweetheart", that we were never, ever to stay at the cottage again! The end of an era!

I'll never, ever forget that feeling of contentment, crossing from mainland Wales over Telford's Menai road bridge, into a very special place, Anglesey!!

51

CHAPTER 12

"WHERE'S OUR GRANDSON, DOROTHY?"

You are possibly thinking that I, as a Carer, am not very good. In Chapter 10, I told you about Dorothy and Alex being lost for hours and now another "lost" grandson. This chapter is not as harrowing for me by a long stretch. Jakson was only missing for minutes but, again, it proves the point that even in the middle stage, you cannot take your eye off an Alzheimer's sufferer for a second. Staying at Dee and Zak's house in Walthamstow, Dorothy and I took Jakson, their son and heir, shopping at Morrison's. Since the trauma of Chapter 10, I had never left Dorothy to walk alone, outside the house. The events of the chapter are absolutely accurate and illustrate the need, never, ever, to have your loved-one out of sight.

Dorothy wanted to push the trolley, so I agreed. We placed Jakson, a lively eighteen-month-old, in the child seat of the trolley. Off we set to find all the bargains.

In Morrison's on Hollinwood Avenue, a drive of less than a mile from "Horner Towers", I know each dedicated position for every item sold there. At this London branch, I just kept my eyes "peeled" to spot the items on my shopping list. I had selected a loaf and placed it in the trolley; Dorothy was stationary, so I turned back to select a packet of muffins which I had overlooked. For how long were Dorothy and Jakson out of sight? Seconds only! But Dorothy had Alzheimer's and I had committed a mighty blunder. Dorothy was standing, more or less in the same place as she had been when I went back for the muffins. However, the shopping trolley and toddler Jakson were gone. "Where's our grandson, Dorothy?" I half shouted. "I don't know", she replied, as though nothing was wrong.

I felt the Adrenalin surging through my body. Stopping a middle-aged lady shopper, I hurriedly explained the situation and ran off, leaving the lady holding Dorothy's hand. Usain Bolt had nothing on me as I raced around Morrison's checking every aisle and corner. Not there! But a trolley and child don't just disappear into thin air! Returning to where Dorothy and the lady were standing, I saw two young male shelf-fillers topping up some tins. Again, I explained breathlessly what had happened, pointing out my wife and saying could they search the store for the trolley with a dark-haired toddler sitting inside. I said I was going to search outside in case the unthinkable had happened and Jakson had been abducted.

Out on the car park shoppers looked on in amazement as I hurtled around, not really knowing where to search on this huge car park.

Nearing sheer exhaustion, I decided to return inside the Supermarket. Dorothy, the lady shopper, Jakson in the shopping trolley, together with the two shop assistants, were standing together in a small group. "Where was he?" I spluttered. It would appear that Dorothy had pushed the trolley, together with Jakson, down to the far corner and through an entrance into the warehouse section. That part of the warehouse was little used and I had only been looking inside the Supermarket. The strips of plastic hanging vertically from this entrance to the warehouse had rendered the trolley and Jakson, invisible to me.

Thanking the lady shopper and the two young assistants profusely, Dorothy, Jakson and I completed the shopping without any further problems.

I cannot emphasize enough, as you, dear reader, go about your caring duties, not to take your eyes off your charge for a second. The most innocent of situations can turn out so very unpleasant for you and your loved one.

A massive point I want to make at this juncture. Dorothy could not remember wheeling Jakson through that entrance into the warehouse section but she could still recall the day we met in 1955!

CHAPTER 13

DOCTOR N. A. MORRIS G. P.

Doctor Morris is one of several doctors at the Failsworth Health Centre. I would think that he is now the Senior Doctor, as he has practiced medicine at the Health Centre for over 30 years.

I remember him commencing his career as a General Practitioner. He is one of those fortunate people who have hardly changed in over three decades. Doctor Morris has the ability to put his patients at ease with consummate skill, long described as a "bedside manner". His genuine friendliness and conscientiousness inspire confidence in his patients. For years, even before Dorothy's wheelchair days, Dr. Morris would already be holding the surgery door open, as I helped my wife towards a chair. He once said, a couple of years ago, that he thought that I knew more about Alzheimer's than he did. I don't know about that, Dr. Morris, but thanks for saying it anyhow.

Once a month, Dr. Morris makes his "regular-as-clockwork" courtesy call. He always telephones me on the previous day, of his intention to visit. I feel as though I'm chatting to a friend when he arrives. If I ever require an emergency visit, I have his permission to telephone reception and leave a message, knowing he will telephone back as soon as possible.

On the occasion of Dorothy's second stroke, I did exactly that and as Dr. Morris was finishing his surgery within minutes, he was at the front door of "Horner Towers" fifteen minutes later. I could see that Dorothy's condition was severe. The doctor quickly confirmed my worse suspicions to be correct and stated that she had, indeed, had a second stroke. He immediately telephoned for an ambulance. Looking back, two years ago, I recall vividly the genuine kindness he displayed. Putting a hand on my shoulder, he said that all was not lost but that I may have to prepare myself for the worst.

Dorothy was in hospital for nine weeks. Having fought off her second, almost fatal, stroke, she is now, as I write Chapter 13 of this book, back in her hospital bed, in the sitting room.

Life goes on, as life does. Dr. Morris continues his house call each month. I and my family feel a tremendous debt of gratitude towards this unique, devoted and very kind Doctor. Thank you Dr. Morris!

CHAPTER 14

THE FUNERAL MEAL WITH A DIFFERENCE

This is the chapter in my book which contains the only anecdotal-type incidents.

Alzheimer's is a horrible, all-consuming disease, where few, if any, humorous events will occur. The incidents I relate here happened in the years 2001/2, when Dorothy was in her seventh year of Alzheimer's. She was in the second stage and "Aricept" was helping her enormously.

My Uncle Henry was 92 when he died in 2003. I liked him very much and he often stayed with Dorothy and me at "Horner Towers" for a full week. He used the sitting room, where Dorothy is now, as a bedroom, because the downstairs toilet faces that room.

The funeral took place in Hull and a hot meal was booked for the funeral party at a local pub/restaurant. After drinks at the bar, we were asked to take our seats in the restaurant section, for a three-course meal. Dorothy could eat using her knife and fork, so no attention was drawn to our table and very few mourners there knew that she had Alzheimer's.

Halfway through the main course Dorothy said she needed the toilet. I took her, and as the toilets were only a few yards from our table I said I would wait outside for her but she insisted I return to my seat because she could see our table.

I was continuing my conversation with my Uncle Ken when I became aware that there was a bit of a commotion on an adjacent table. To the absolute surprise of the mourners sitting on that table, Dorothy suddenly sitting down in an empty seat, which had been vacated by a gentleman who had gone to purchase drinks at the bar, must have been bizarre to say the least. Matters were

58

made much worse by the fact that Dorothy had picked up the knife and fork of this gentleman and started eating his meal without a visible care in the world. I was out of my chair and across the room to Dorothy before you could say: "What's for dessert?" Furnishing the open-mouthed diner with a clean knife and fork, I led my wife back to her seat next to me. I'm certain that the recipient of this touchingly humorous experience, or anyone else in the restaurant who witnessed the incident, will have given an account of the event on numerous occasions. Uncle Henry would have chuckled, I'm sure, had he been present.

Round about this period, in stage two of Dorothy's illness, a couple more things occurred which are worthy of a mention.

We'd driven over to the Lancashire coast for a relaxing day out. Dorothy said she needed "toilet", her one-word request to "spend a penny". Incontinence hadn't yet struck, otherwise I would have had the changing bag with me and we would have used the Disabled Toilet. Dorothy appeared to walk in the general direction of the "Ladies". I didn't need the "Gents", so I said I'd wait outside for her. At this juncture, I should have practiced what I preach: with Alzheimer's always expect the unexpected".

Standing outside the red-brick building, I turned around on hearing footsteps, to see Dorothy coming out of the "Gents". Before I could say anything, she said, "They are the strangest Ladies toilets I've ever been in. The toilets are O.K. but there's wash hand basins as normal and some smaller ones half-way up the wall without taps". Luckily, no gentlemen were in the toilets during that three or four minutes but next time, I wouldn't leave things to chance!

A few weeks after the funeral meal in Hull, a similar type of amusing incident occurred during our evening meal. Dorothy and I were well into a hot meal when the telephone rang. I was expecting a call and said, "Won't be long, back in two minutes". I was a little longer than two minutes, maybe five, but I didn't want my unfinished meal to get cold. It didn't get cold as it worked out but I was not the one to finish eating it. Dorothy, bless her, finished her own meal and in my absence, polished off mine too. At least she had used her own cutlery on this occasion. How we laughed!

The last of this miniseries of humorous experiences happened in our local Morrison's store. Good job the staff there knew of Dorothy's disability, otherwise we could have been led off in handcuffs - only joking! Dorothy loved walking round Morrison's helping with the weekly shop. At the checkout she would take the items out of the trolley and place them on the conveyor belt and I would "bag up" the groceries, at the other end.

On this particular day I was aware that she was by-passing the conveyor belt and carrying items, one at a time, to the bagging up area. I don't know if the check out lady had noticed but I started to chuckle and asked her to abort the till roll and start again, this time with Dorothy packing the groceries into bags and me in charge of the conveyor belt.

Again, I repeat: "with Alzheimer's, expect the unexpected".

CHAPTER 15

RAINY SHOPPING DAY AND UNINVITED GUESTS AT "HORNER TOWERS"

Just because I'm a carer does not exclude people from wanting to be unpleasant or do something unpleasant. This chapter is a few years down the line from the humorous incident at Morrison's in the previous chapter. But it did involve me shopping alone on a horribly rainy Manchester day and what transpired because of that.

The rain had set in with a vengeance and I decided to leave Dorothy at home, safe and dry, whilst I dashed out for a quick shop. Even when I took her with me, because she now could hardly walk, I used to leave her secure in the car. But Dorothy would have been saturated, just getting her into my car. However, much happened in the twenty-five minutes I was away. Read on!

I was aware from some distance away that a Police car was parked outside my house. My heart quickened immediately and was beating fifty to the dozen as I swung right into the driveway. The seven-feet-high wooden gate between the house and the garage was ajar and obviously damaged. A break-in I was thinking. All this in a twenty-five minute absence away from home. The last time I had had a break in I waited over five hours for the Police to put in an appearance. Today was truly an Olympic standard.

All this in five seconds, as I was about to open the front door, to check that Dorothy was safe and unharmed. The key was turning in the lock as I heard a voice bellow, "Oh, you're back then are you"? Turning my head abruptly, two PCs appeared, as if out of nowhere. I had noticed that they were not sitting in their car, as I had passed it seconds earlier. They must have been to the rear of the house. The very tall PC was the "Shouter". Even as I led the way into the lounge where Dorothy was sitting serenely sucking her thumb, he was still shouting but now it was, "Why have you left your disabled wife alone in the house?" I asked him to lower his voice as he was frightening Dorothy. He did so but only about ten decibels. I put my question to the other PC, who at that stage had not said a word. "Who telephoned 999 for you to be here?" "Your neighbour noticed you leaving without your wife", he replied. This officer spoke in a rational voice. The other was still bellowing, "You've no right to leave someone alone in a wheelchair!" Needless to say it was PC "Shouter" who had battered open the side gate. I said that I would send him the bill for the damage but, at a later date, I repaired it myself.

I quickly explained the reason why I had not taken Dorothy with me that morning and that I had only been away for twenty-five minutes. I went on to say that every morning I attended to my wife's toiletry needs first and took her downstairs to sit safely in her wheelchair. It was then my turn to perform my ablutions, which, on average, took about half-an-hour. At this stage of her illness Dorothy was left every day and nothing untoward had ever happened.

I then ordered PC "Shouter" to go and sit in his car as he was showing absolutely zero respect to a Carer and senior citizen. Amazingly, he left, and PC "Nice Guy" and I were able to have a quiet chat.

He asked me lots of questions about Alzheimer's and I made us a cup of tea. Before leaving he said that, with respect, he would have to report the fact that they had been called out to the home of a disabled person. It was Police policy he said, apologetically, to inform the Social Services.

He left, but within the hour, three staff members of Manchester Social Services, including the Head of Department, arrived at my front door. They looked disapprovingly at me, three middle-aged ladies, all with their hearts in the right place though. Within five minutes I had explained, as I had to PC "Nice Guy", that Dorothy was left every morning, as I attended to my bathroom requisites. They accepted the explanation graciously but were appalled at my neighbour's action of calling out the Police.

An interesting day, no doubt at all. I'd made a friend of one policeman but an enemy of another one. But my real enemy was much closer to home.

CHAPTER 16

"SORRY, DOROTHY ONLY HAS 18 MONTHS TO LIVE"

After Dorothy was diagnosed with Alzheimer's, we attended a clinic at North Manchester General Hospital every three months. A Consultant of Psychopathology would set her simple mental tests to ascertain the deterioration of her brain.

Once the initial CT scan has diagnosed evidence of Alzheimer's, it is not necessary for any further CT scans. The Consultant overrules whatever our GPs opinion is, with respect to the introduction or removal of the supply of Aricept, on prescription. This, as previously mentioned, is a wonderful medication which will lengthen the period of stage two of Alzheimer's.

Admiral nurses are wonderful, dedicated ladies. Their hearts are in the right place and they are there to help us, the carers. That is not to say they wouldn't help our loved one or give advice but primarily they are the "Carer's nurse". You may be thinking by now, for what exactly are Admiral nurses employed? They are the equivalent of what MacMillan nurses are to cancer Carers. They advise in the main but their one-hour visit is mainly to cheer up the Carer. It works too! My Admiral nurse was of a cheerful disposition and the one-hour visits passed all too quickly, until in 2002, my Admiral nurse, on her arrival at "Horner Towers", informed me of some startling news. She told me that Dorothy had only 18 months to live! I could hardly believe what she had said but she was adamant that her prognosis was correct.

Now, let me tell you that prior to the Admiral nurse's prognosis, neither the Consultant nor Doctor Morris had ever spoken in terms of how long Dorothy had to live. On the one occasion I asked Doctor Morris, possibly circa 2004, how long could Dorothy withstand the effects of Alzheimer's, he refused to commit himself. He went on to say that Alzheimer victims did not pass away because of Alzheimer's but with it. Another virulent illness like a stroke or pneumonia could be the cause of death.

Well, here we are in 2012 and I still have my lovely wife, albeit two strokes later and well into stage three of Alzheimer's.

My advice is, that if you have an Admiral nurse calling at your home, don't ever talk about her ideas as to the time of your loved one's demise. It is better by far that no one, not even medical experts, should speculate on such a subject.

CHAPTER 17

MALARIA - LUCKY TO BE ALIVE!

Dorothy and I contracted malaria in March 1998. The memories of the severity of this disease are branded in my psyche. Malaria is a killer, claiming two million lives, mainly in the third world, every year. It seems incomprehensible that man has walked on the moon but a female mosquito, albeit diseased, defies scientists' attempts to eradicate malaria.

In the 1950s DDT was invented and initially appeared to have beaten the accursed insect. Not for so very long! Subsequent attempts with even more powerful chemicals have failed. If travellers venture to areas of the globe, where these sick, female mosquitoes can bite and pass on their infected fluids, they must take precautions in the form of a course of anti-malaria tablets started weeks beforehand.

Dorothy and I arrived in Johannesburg, South Africa, to spend several weeks with our good friends, Doreen and Brian Perry. It was February 1998 and Dorothy had been taking Aricept for almost a year and was in fine form. Doreen and Brian met us at Jan Smuts' Airport. The thought of the lovely times ahead made all four of us smile with happiness as Doreen and Brian told us about the many places we were to visit.

Dorothy and I had talked of visiting Victoria Falls in Zimbabwe weeks before we left for Jo'burg. We had time aplenty to spend a full week there but Doreen and Brian informed us that they had seen Victoria Falls twice already and would we mind going by ourselves. "Of course not," I replied. The weather in South Africa was superb, just as I remembered from our world trip three years previously. We went here, there and everywhere, enjoying each others' company and splendid meals, in the evenings, eaten in a plethora of fantastic restaurants.

The day eventually arrived for the Zimbabwe trip. Brian and Doreen waved us off at the airport and a few hours later we arrived at our hotel, built entirely of timber, known as a "holiday lodge". We were welcomed by a male member of the hotel staff, dressed in the full native war regalia of a chieftain, complete with war paint, spear and machete. The following day we posed for photographs by his side. Jo'burg was cool compared to the furnace-like heat of this arid area.

The days passed pleasantly. On two occasions we visited Victoria Falls. The views along the walkways were breathtaking - the constant rainbows, like paintings in all their vibrant seven colours. Soaked to the skin, the experience was like a cooling shower that was a delight to participate in. On returning to the entrance area, families of monkeys amused us for several minutes until we realised our clothes and hair were bone dry.

Victoria Falls in Zimbabwe is very close to Victoria Falls in Zambia. It's just a matter of walking across Victoria Bridge. That in itself is quite an experience. Arriving at the border between Zimbabwe and Zambia, I realised that our passports were back at the lodge. The official at the control was not concerned about passports, just the entrance fee to explore their side of Victoria Falls. "Only Zambian dollars" muttered the officer, "no Zimbabwean dollars" All we had was the latter but I always carry single US dollar bills for tipping. "Ah yes," beamed he, "American dollars good". I had only six dollars and he stated that it was five each. "Just give us one ticket between us", I urged, "You keep the one dollar for yourself". Result! So if the Zambian balance of payments was down in 1998, now you know why! I'm sorry to say this, Zimbabwe, but the Zambian side of Victoria Falls is the better; truly astonishing. The rainbows, the width of the falls, everything.

That evening Dorothy and I had an outdoor meal at a local restaurant. All the entertainment was performed by local people in native costume. The "home brew" beer was absolutely undrinkable but the wine was superb. Was that a mosquito nibbling at my ankle?

During the flight back to Jo'burg I became aware of how thirsty I was, drinking at least three glasses of iced water. Dorothy drank just one glass. A beaming Doreen and Brian were waiting for us at "Arrivals" and informed us that we were off to Durban the following day to stay at their son, Dave's, seaside holiday home.

The journey was very interesting, well over 300 miles and I was able to take my turn at the wheel. Jo'burg is on a high plateau, so it was downhill all the way.

In the evening, after unpacking, we went for a meal of fish and chips. I recall that my appetite was not as robust as normal and I could only manage to eat half the meal. Also, much to Brian's amazement, I could only manage to drink one bottle of "Castle" lager, South Africa's favourite tipple. Dorothy's appetite was fine, she finished off my fish and I thought I was feeling a bit "off". due to the long journey and high temperatures. During the first night at the holiday chalet, I was awakened twice with severe backache but it had passed by dawn.

We planned out our day and looked forward to pleasant hours in each other's company. I joked to Brian that I would teach him to swim. He had served his National Service in the Navy but couldn't swim. He always said there were life boats on board and it was now "a little too late in the day".

We all enjoyed Durban and the surrounding area but my backache was becoming much worse, combined with loss of appetite and severe sweating.

Doreen and Brian invited a couple of friends round for drinks on the last night at the chalet. For days now, I'd been putting on an act that I felt reasonably well but, during the middle of the laughing and joking I needed to lie down for an hour, my backache was so bad.

The following day, Wednesday, 18th March 1998, we set off back to Jo'burg. I felt awful and I couldn't do my stint at the wheel. The air conditioning system stopped working after the first hour and we all were longing for the journey to end. Eventually, we arrived back in Benoni, on the outskirts of Jo'burg and the Perry's home. I knew then something must be really wrong with me, to feel so dreadful.

Dorothy, at this stage, appeared to be OK, apart from her Alzheimer's, of course.

Thursday, 19th March dawned. I lay in bed wondering what the hell was wrong with me. I'd been disguising how I felt for about four or five days now and I didn't think I could keep up the act much longer. Dorothy awoke and needed the toilet. I took her and we both showered. I dressed her, feeling like death. A walk around the massive garden left me feeling no better. Doreen shouted from the patio that breakfast was ready and Dorothy said she didn't feel very hungry but she ate it all. I pushed my egg and bacon around my plate but ate a slice of toast. Liquid was all I needed, cups of tea, fruit juice and water by the glassful.

Brian worked on Thursdays at his little part-time job. He suggested I watch cricket on TV - South Africa v England, as I looked off colour. Doreen had prepared some sandwiches for our lunch. She was to visit her younger daughter and proceed from there for her computer lesson. "Back for tea time", she yelled, shutting the front door behind her. Dorothy ate two sandwiches at mid-day and I made us a drink of tea. I tried to eat but couldn't swallow. Just sitting in an easy chair was intolerable. I'd bought some Alka Seltzer in Durban but they didn't help at all. A feeling of absolute nausea swept over me and the pain in my back and limbs was excruciating. I asked Dorothy how she felt and she replied that she just felt very hot. "No pain sweetheart?" I asked, "No, just hot", she replied. Suddenly, I had to dash for the bathroom! A nauseous, disgusting reaction inside me, causing retching, leading to vomiting.

Sweat dripped onto the floor. "Are you all right?" questioned Dorothy, "I could hear you being sick". My next dash to the bathroom was even more dramatic. The "trots" causing my dash to be not a second too soon. I suddenly realised, on returning to the TV lounge, that I was lurching along, hardly able to stay on my feet.

Doreen arrived home just after 5 o'clock. I immediately asked her if she would take me to the Doctor's and informed her of my afternoon's "activities". Brian was due home about 6 o'clock. Sensible Doreen supplied a towel, in case I was sick again, which I was. I knew something was seriously wrong with me, but what?

The local Benoni Health Centre is about two miles from Doreen and Brian's home. I couldn't walk the few yards from the car park to the Surgery, but Doreen brought a wheel chair to me. The Health Service in South Africa is strictly private, there is no free NHS but the hours you can visit a doctor are from 6 in the morning until 10 in the evening, every day of the week. Very civilised. I think Dr. Dyson had made up his mind the moment he saw me that I had malaria. However, he took a blood sample and telephoned for a motorbike messenger to have the sample tested. The result was telephoned back to him twenty minutes later - definitely malaria. Dr. Dyson asked if Doreen would run me to the main Johannesburg hospital to save time, by not ordering an ambulance. He merely telephoned my imminent arrival.

Very soon I was the fourth patient in a four-man ward. My treatment started immediately; tubes here, there and everywhere. At least, I was thinking, if with more than a little confusion, I now knew what my problem was and I was receiving treatment. Home and hosed?" Little did I realise then, but I was starting on a very long road to recovery!

I recall babbling away about my car needing an MOT but I soon drifted off into a deep sleep. Suddenly, I realised I was being shaken by the shoulder. Looking up through half-closed eyes, I was aware of Dorothy, Doreen and Brian standing over me. It seemed ages since my admission to the ward but, in actual fact, it was only 8.00 p.m. Doreen said that at tea-time at their house Dorothy had been sick and felt awful. They took her to

70

Dr. Dyson's Surgery and it was confirmed that she too had malaria, but thankfully it was not at such an advanced stage as mine.

The upshot of this was that Dorothy and I could be in a family room. Lots of space for two hospital beds with an adjacent en suite bathroom. I wasn't aware of being there until the early hours of Friday, 20th March. There was much activity around my bed and lots of people coming and going. At daybreak, with nurses bringing and emptying bedpans, changing empty transfusion containers and constant bed baths to remove the endless sweat, I became aware of the Nursing Sister standing, looking intently at me.

"We were very concerned about you, Mr. Horner, during the night", she said. "Surely not, Sister", I replied, "Not now I'm here in hospital being treated". The Sister gave a wry smile and answered, "Even in hospital we lose quite a few malaria patients, who have left the treatment too late to be saved."

A few days later, when Dorothy and I were slowly recovering, she informed me that had I gone to bed on Thursday night, not having seen Doctor Dyson, I would not have woken up on Friday morning. My life would have ebbed away during the small hours. Thankfully, because Dorothy's condition was never as serious as mine, due to being bitten a few days after me, she reacted more quickly to the treatment and subsequently her pain and suffering were less than that of "full on" malaria.

I cannot speak too highly of the nursing standards Dorothy and I experienced in the Malaria Unit of Johannesburg's main hospital. The imperturbable Doctor Dyson visited us twice daily and I could feel the empathy within him.

After sixteen days we were discharged to convalesce under the care of Doreen. Nothing was too much trouble for her. She was kindness personified! Dear Doreen died in 2010 from the effects of a severe heart attack. Her memory will live on forever. RIP Doreen.

Eventually, five weeks later than scheduled, we arrived home in Manchester. We flew Business Class because there were no standard flights available for two more weeks. All that lovely, sumptuous food and drink. Dorothy had a glass of champagne and some fresh salmon but all I had for the twelve-hour flight was Perrier water and painkillers. The lovely tans we had acquired had long gone by the time we arrived home.

I knew malaria was a mega killer but I never, ever thought that Dorothy and I would fall foul of it. Dorothy very quickly shook off the effects of the disease but it took me almost two years to be anywhere near normal. The attacks of pain were staggering in their intensity and at one period, a year after arriving home, my weight had plummeted from my usual 11 stones 7 pounds to 7 stones 4 pounds.

Malaria could have caused our premature deaths. I am so glad that fourteen years and four months on, I am still able to be Dorothy's Carer!

CHAPTER 18

OUR FRIEND JASON, THE GENTLE GIANT

Fourteen years ago, a neighbour from across the road gave me a petition to sign. "What's all this about?" I asked him. He explained to me that No. 38, the big house on the corner, was to be a home for mentally challenged males. "We don't want men like that round here", he muttered. "I can't, and I won't sign this", I replied "Dorothy is mentally challenged, remember she has Alzheimer's". The petition was duly sent to Manchester Town Hall, but to no avail; No.38 Hawthorn Road became a residential home.

A few weeks later, totally refurbished the "Big House", as I call it, opened. I was aware of new faces in the area but just got on with my own job as Dorothy's Carer.

One day, my doorbell rang and on answering it I was looking up into the face of the tallest young man I had ever seen. He must have been over 30 stones in weight. The second man was of average height, like myself. My immediate thought was that they didn't look like Jehovah's Witnesses. The larger man held out his hand to shake and said "I'm Jason, I live at No. 38 and what I do is clean cars, £2 a car". I shook his hand and also that of his carer saying, "I clean my own car thanks Jason but if I ever need you, I know you live at No.38".

I was to discover later, that at that time Jason weighed 34 stones and is 6 feet 9 inches tall. A veritable giant, but a gentle one!

I've never really got to know what Jason's problems are. As stated, he is very large but Dorothy and I found him to be so

73

likeable and very friendly. He has a self-contained flat on the top floor of No. 38 - I refer to it as his "penthouse suite".

Jason requires constant supervision because of his mental capacity but once he trusts and likes you, you're "forever friends". Most of the people on Hawthorn Road shun him. Surely they can see after many years, that he is not a threat. Are they intimidated by his size? Or is it the same reason that they ignore Dorothy, because of Alzheimer's? Any illness of the brain, eh?

Over the years, with permission from the Care Home Leader, Jason has assisted me with outdoor jobs. He loves to help. I make him home-made fish and chips and as many cooling drinks as he requires. He always asks how Dorothy is. She has been bedridden now for over six years and he says, "It's not fair. She doesn't deserve this" and kisses her on her forehead. I'll never forget your kindness Jason, but life hasn't been very fair to you, my friend.

Yesterday, 26 July, was Jason's birthday. He goes along the road with hand-written invitations to his party but rarely does anyone bother to attend. You are missing a real treat, my neighbours! The Carers at No.38 put on a buffet-type spread for us. Really exceptional food! Thanks staff! We all sang "Happy Birthday" and I started everyone off with "For he's a jolly good fellow". Jason enjoyed every moment of his special day. Jason is now 38 and I'm 74 but I have total respect for him; he's my equal. He just needs help with stuff.

Today, Saturday, 28 July, I went to his penthouse suite at 10.30 a.m. and made him eggs and bacon on toast. I also made him an omelette for later on. He likes me to prepare any fresh fruit he has purchased from Morrison's. This morning it was fresh pineapples and bananas. I visit him every Saturday morning at 10.30 a.m. and prepare some food. Apart from the fact he's a friend, I feel as though I'm putting something back into life that I've taken out. Until 2 years ago, Jason couldn't tell the time. I taught him at my home with a clock made from cardboard. It took him many

74

months of weekly visits. Well done Jason! His reward - a large kitchen clock from Morrison's.

Just a few words about Jason's weight. Fourteen years ago he weighed 34 stones, now he weighs 26 stones. His weight is not related to the amount of food he eats. I've noticed over the years that he eats less than me and I'm 11 stones 7 pounds. His health problems have made him into a very large man and, of course, affected him intellectually. Enjoy your life Jason! Dorothy and I have enjoyed having known you!

CHAPTER 19

THE HORROR OF DOUBLE INCONTINENCE

No amount of mental preparation is sufficient for the day incontinence by faeces strikes. It will inevitably happen to your loved one. This occurs at the start of, or during, stage 3. You, the Carer, as in my case, hope and pray that your loved one will be spared this grossly, horrifying indignity. But incontinence wins! It is, without any doubt, the main reason why Carers finally admit their loved ones to a nursing home. It is the last straw that "breaks the camel's/Carer's back".

Prior to July 2004, Dorothy had always, without fail, asked for the toilet. This was whether it was for a "number one" or a "number two", as we both referred to these bodily functions. On this momentous evening in July 2004, I went upstairs for a quick shower and was on my way downstairs, six or seven minutes later, when I realised that a "number two" had happened - but not in the downstairs toilet! With my heart beating like a bongo drum, I stepped through the open doorway into the lounge. Total devastation assaulted my gaze!

Dorothy had had a large bowel movement and realised she had done wrong. In addition to the faeces being in her hair and on her face and hands, she had tried to hide it under the sofa, in plant pots, wiping her hands on the curtains, wallpaper, easy chairs, her clothing and treading the horrendous mess into the carpet.

I must have stood in shock, for what seemed like five minutes, but realistically was only about twenty seconds. I am a regular dreamer; every night I dream in brilliant Technicolor and I said to myself, "I'm dreaming all this". But I wasn't - a living nightmare was everywhere I looked.

"Deep breathing, deep breaths", I remember saying to myself. "Don't move Dorothy", I mumbled. "Stand still please". Making a pathway of newspaper, I quickly undressed her, and leaving everything on the floor, led my apologising wife upstairs to the bathroom. Hardly able to speak, I quickly changed the bathwater and rinsed Dorothy's hair for the third time, knowing that she was now 100% clean. And so to bed: for my wife, that was.

Re-entering the lounge, I almost gagged at the sight, to which no one should ever be subjected. If Alzheimer's is the "embezzler" of lives, then this heinous extension to the illness is unique in its horror. Not content with stealing years of my loved one's life, now Alzheimer's was taking away Dorothy's dignity. Hardly aware that I was sobbing, as I refilled countless bowls of cleaning water, I thought of the day we met: 5 December 1955. My sweetheart, my lovely, pretty, funny, witty, charismatic Dorothy had been reduced to this ....

My washing machine earned its keep that night. Two cycles for Dorothy's clothing and her sandals. Also, the curtains. I looked up at the stars as I pegged out my washing at 2.00 a.m. Not far to go now. Slowly and with absolute care, I removed every last bit of evidence of what had taken place at 9.00 p.m. The wallpaper, painted in washable vinyl, was now spotless, the carpet now smelt like a flower garden. the sofa and easy chairs were back to pristine appearance.

I recall looking at the lounge clock; it was 2.50 a.m. I had finished! I was so exhausted I could hardly stand up but one last thing remained - a long, hot shower!

The morning after the night before! Every muscle in my body ached from the exertion of just a few hours ago. I brought us both a cup and tea and we chatted as usual. "Don't worry about what happened last night Dorothy", I said gently. She turned to look at me, saying, "Why, what happened last night?" "Nothing important, sweetheart", I replied.

That morning, after bringing in the washing, we called at "Boots" chemist and I purchased several dozen incontinence pads. A few weeks later I discovered that Dorothy could have them on prescription

With hindsight, and a crystal ball, I should have seen incontinence approaching. Maybe I didn't want to believe it was going to happen to my loved one. There are moments which mark your life. Moments when you realise nothing will ever be the same and that time is divided into two parts; before this and after this. Incontinence; maybe the most horrendous facet of Alzheimer's ?

Christmas 1992 (Pre-Alzheimer's)

Two years after diagnosis 1996

Dorothy with her daughters and grandchildren 2002

By the lake 2003

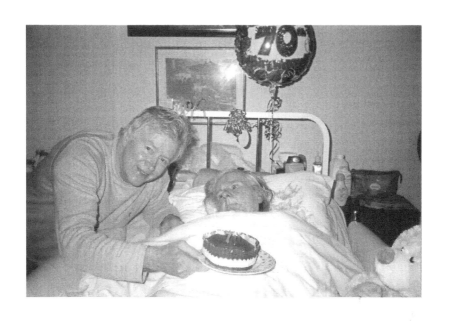

Dorothy's 70th birthday 2008

CHAPTER 20

A CHECK-UP WITH
MY DENTIST

Hardly a wonderful experience but the practice I visited twice a year, performed an excellent, very necessary service.

The surgery is situated a short car drive from "Horner Towers". Twice a year I had my check-up. Possibly a filling or an X-ray and always a word of encouragement from the dentist, "Look after your teeth", (sensible words)

"It's so worthwhile if you do and replace your toothbrush regularly".

Dorothy's dentist was in Manchester City Centre, on High Street. During the twenty-odd years of working in the city, she'd always had Ms. Coates as her dentist. Ms Coates was aware, of course, that Dorothy suffered from Alzheimer's and was kindness itself. She went to great lengths explaining to me what Dorothy's treatment entailed.

My dentist would have accepted Dorothy as her patient, but having been so long with Ms. Coates, she said she'd like to remain with, "My lovely, friendly dentist," as she described Ms. Coates.

Dorothy would sit contentedly in the waiting room whilst I had my check-ups or ensuing treatment. The receptionist was aware that my wife had Alzheimer's but never, ever made any attempt at small talk with her. This I did not mind. Not everyone wishes to engage in conversation with someone with Alzheimer's.

So, one appointment day in 2003, my name was called. I smiled at Dorothy, squeezed her hand and said, "Won't be long, sweetheart, it's only an inspection". I strode off to the open surgery door but, as I drew level with the receptionist, I said, "Please keep your eye on Dorothy". I don't know why, as I had never done this in all the years that she had accompanied me. Little did I know I was to pay heavily for that slight request.

Three minutes later I was out of the surgery - clean bill of health for my teeth this time. I was pleased, like anyone else, I hate having a filling.

The receptionist had a form for me to sign and I had my Visa card in my hand, ready to pay for the dentist's time. But what was this the receptionist was saying to me? "Don't bring your wife here again, caring is not on my work contract." What I had requested was irrelevant to the receptionist's contract. It was a "throw away" request. Besides, Dorothy hadn't moved an inch. I could feel the anger rising within me but we left without me uttering one word in defence.

The following day I decided, mostly because I'm so protective of Dorothy, that I would return to the dental surgery and ask the receptionist why just keeping an "eye-out" for an Alzheimer's victim was too much to ask. I'd left Dorothy in the car but the receptionist was just as adamant as the previous day. "I'm not a care worker" she trilled, "I'm a receptionist and don't bring her again!"

Not wishing to make any more of the issue, I thought that was the end of it. Not so! A few days later I received a letter from the dentist stating that I had caused trouble with her staff and that I had been "struck off" her patients' list.

I did reply to the letter stating that she was a better person than this and that "the tail was wagging the dog". Also, that had I been a private patient, I didn't think I would have been "struck off".

Ms. Coates had opened a new surgery in Rochdale and her list was full so I commenced treatment with a really good dentist in Manchester City Centre. Before starting my first treatment, I asked the receptionist would she be able to keep an eye on my wife as she had Alzheimer's. She looked at me in a puzzled sort of way and without sarcasm said, "Is this a trick question,? that's part of my job".

On my last appointment with Jonathan, who really is an excellent dentist, an incident occurred with my car and a traffic warden (The red-caps). I had a blue disability badge for Dorothy duly displayed, as the rules demand, but on our return, I found I had received a parking ticket.

There are insufficient disability parking bays in Manchester City Centre. Not wishing to have to push Dorothy's wheelchair too far in the rain, I had parked behind a lorry, about 400 metres from St. Anne's Square. The problem for me was that the lorry was parked over a painted sign on the road: "No parking, for unloading only". I really did not see the sign until I returned 45 minutes later, the lorry by then having driven off.

Initially, the "powers-that-be" refused to cancel the fine but I persevered. In my second request to have the fine quashed I stated that I would rather go to prison than pay it and said that a disabled person would be their sole responsibility during my stay in Strangeways Prison. Result - I was given a warning and that, as they say, was that.

Early in the following year, 2006, Dorothy had her first stroke, so in fact 2005 was the last year I visited a dentist. Leaving my loved one alone, to travel to Manchester City Centre, at the moment, is a risk too far.

Yes! Teeth can be a problem from babyhood all the way through to old age!

CHAPTER 21

DOROTHY HAS A STROKE IN NORTH MANCHESTER GENERAL HOSPITAL

February is renowned for being the worst month of winter. Most of our snow arrives then and in 2006, Dorothy and I were feeling the effects of an exceptionally cold spell, as elderly people do. Dorothy went everywhere now, outside the car, in her wheelchair. Inside "Horner Towers", she either sat in an easy chair with the raised legs, or stayed in the wheelchair, as at meal times.

On a freezing cold morning early in February, I took Dorothy for an appointment with Dr Morris. Getting Dorothy into the car and out again at the Health Centre took more effort than usual that morning. Dr Morris held the surgery door open for us and I sat as he did the usual blood pressure and heart tests. Dorothy's blood pressure was up, but not significantly. The Doctor thought I looked jaded and suggested that I apply for some respite care at North Manchester General Hospital. Dorothy had stayed in "Orchard Unit" there, two or three times but "White Moss", a Social Services residential home in Blackley, had now closed down.

Arriving at the hospital, I was aware, once again, how reluctant Dorothy was to assist me in getting her into the wheelchair. Going along the corridors I became conscious of the fact she had not spoken a single word since leaving the Health Centre. I thought perhaps that she was feeling cold and I knew someone would make us a cup of tea in "Orchard Unit".

It was good to see friendly, familiar faces at the Unit but Anne, the Charge Nurse, informed me that they could not offer any respite care for Dorothy because all the rooms were now 100% residential. I accepted this information with good grace. Even

87

during four or five days respite care, I missed Dorothy so much that I would be visiting her after the first day. No respite then, no "big deal". The cup of tea was reviving but Dorothy hardly drank hers and even during the five minutes of being fussed over she never spoke a word.

It was now 12.25 p.m. and we were just about to take our leave. Dorothy was slightly behind my line of vision but the nurses were standing facing us. Suddenly, their faces showed a look of alarm. Anne said, "Oh, my God, someone get the oxygen mask!" I turned my head to look at whom the cause of this concern was directed. It was Dorothy - she was having a violent stroke! Eyes bulging, her arms and legs shaking, we placed her in the recovery position and within seconds oxygen was administered. I'm certain that had I been at home, the vital help required to keep my loved one alive would have arrived too late by the time the ambulance came. The oxygen and the intensive care procedures saved Dorothy's life during the "Golden Hour". I was in a total daze: was this to be the last day of her life?

Over and over again, the same thought pounded through my head. Alzheimer's victims die with Alzheimer's, not because of it! The two main causes of death are stroke and pneumonia. Dorothy had done so well for 12 years but the end had to come sometime and this was a massive stroke. I wasn't ready yet for her loss but I wouldn't ever be, I knew that. In Intensive Care Dorothy was still unconscious, but now tubes were everywhere, in her arms and up her nostrils. An oxygen mask covered her lower face. The monitors over the bed were measuring every heartbeat and any changes in her condition.

The Sister in charge of Intensive Care came to the bedside and beckoned me towards the nurses' room. "Come back later", she said softly, "We may have more encouraging news then".

Thoughts were pounding away in my head. I'd arrived at the Hospital hours before and now I would be driving home without Dorothy. I could feel the tears behind my eyes and the lump in my throat made breathing quite difficult. The Sister, sensing my

88

emotional turmoil, walked two steps towards me and hugged my shaking body. I exploded in a giant sob, hot tears coursing down my cheeks. That wonderful Sister was trained for moments like this. Her gentle, kind voice calmed me down, calmed me into accepting what had happened , as the coping mechanism, which had suddenly taken over my body and mind commenced.

On the way home I called at my elder son's house. I asked him to inform his brother of the events of the day. Immediately on returning home, I rang both my daughters in London. They would arrive the following day by train.

My trademark is optimism and I realised that I would need to peddle optimism avidly during the coming days.

The next day I met my daughters at Piccadilly Station at 10.00 a.m. They'd made an early start. I brought them up to speed on what was happening. Concern was etched on their faces. Oh for a magic wand but I'm just their Dad and I can't control anything. Straight on to the hospital. Dorothy was still comatose and looked just the same as when I had visited with my sons the previous night. We stayed by the bedside until turned 1.00 p.m., then returned home for a quick meal. The house seemed empty without Dorothy - her wheelchair stood forlornly in the lounge. Little did I know that she would never, ever sit in it again.

Back to the hospital by 2.30 p.m. to be greeted by the lovely, serene Sister who had been so kind to me the previous day. We all realised that Dorothy's life hung by a thread but it came as a sledge hammer blow when the Sister asked if Dorothy would appreciate the last rites or the blessing, depending on her religion. I immediately said that my wife would want the blessing if she was able to communicate.

The blessing was a uniquely moving experience for me and my daughters. We said our goodbyes, arms around one another, unabashed tears falling from our eyes. The Minister was marvellous. I was thinking, as he took his leave, that he would have performed this perfunctory service for chronically sick people, hundreds or thousands of times. The enormity of the experience and what the blessing represented left me feeling exhausted. On the way home we all three agreed that if anyone could fight their way out of this trauma, it was Dorothy, my wife, the Mum to our children and the Grandma to our grandchildren.

Liz and Dee returned to London five days later. Dorothy was showing slight signs of improvement but was still in Intensive Care. The staff on duty in that Unit were devoted to their profession. Nothing was too much trouble and their attitude to visitors was of the highest order.

Slowly, very slowly, Dorothy came back from death's door. It was more than three months before she was discharged. A hospital bed was assembled in our sitting room and very quickly it came to resemble a hospital side room For six months my daily care for Dorothy was a morning bed bath, nightdress change and pad plus three more pad changes during the course of the day. Bed linen was changed if soiled and always twice a week if not.

Let me stress to you, dear reader, that what I did for those six months is not to be attempted by a lady Carer. It is really too much for a male Carer but age and the individual's strength and mind set will decide that for you. Where there's a will there's a way!

Dorothy has no use in her body except for her fingers, which she sucks incessantly along with her thumb. At that time, over six years ago, she could still swallow food but everything had to be blended and very small teaspoonfuls only, to be fed to her.

This was a different, much different type of caring to what I had been administering for the previous twelve years. Gone were the monthly trips down to London to stay at our daughters' homes. Gone were the weekly shopping trips to Morrisons, walks in the park, walks around Hollingworth Lake. Gone forever! Dorothy's world now consisted of that one room. The only movement she experienced was the "log roll" from right to left or left to right as I rolled her body to wash her and secure her pad. The stroke had all but ended her ability to speak. Just "yes" and "no" and the occasional gobbledegook. Such is the stuff of life, a severe stroke, if it doesn't kill, then it will maim.

After six months of caring for Dorothy by myself, I was burnt out with exhaustion. The nerve-racking day-after-day routine was making me ill. The answer lay in private care. There isn't an NHS equivalent to this service, which is not to be confused with District Nurses who call daily, or once a month, to check out a patient, as in Dorothy's case.

I started a care package for Dorothy which comprised an hour's caring from 8.00 - 9.00 a.m., half an hour 12.00 - 12.30 p.m., 7.00 - 7.30 p.m., seven days a week. I did the 11.00 p.m. pad change myself.

Now I was to find out about true friendship. False friends stayed away; our true, sincere friends still called to visit us.

CHAPTER 22

DOROTHY HAS A SECOND STROKE

For four years Dorothy lay there, unaware of the changing of the seasons, the visits of our grandchildren, friends and family, and, to be quite honest, absolutely anything at all. I consoled myself and everyone who came to visit Dorothy, that she would not be aware that week in, month out, she lay prostrate in our sitting room. "How do you arrive at that?" or words to that effect, they would ask. My explanation was simple in the extreme. Dorothy for over two years, asked me every few seconds, several hundred times a day, "Will I always have Alzheimer's?" She kept asking because she would forget she had asked thirty seconds earlier.

Lying in bed 24/7 is a similar situation. When she wakes in the morning, she will not be aware that she has spent all yesterday in bed, and, of course, countless other yesterdays. Her attention span is seconds only, no retention whatsoever. No recall of yesterday, last week or last year. Everything always in the present, just that moment in time.

Dr. Morris had this wonderful ability to make me feel confident that Dorothy was safe under his care. He visited once a month and stated categorically that if ever I felt she needed an emergency visit, he would be there ASAP.

Such an occasion arose in March 2010. The 7.30 a.m. care team had just left and I moved into Dorothy's room to spoon feed her breakfast. She just wasn't interested in swallowing, keeping the same mouthful and rolling it around with lips tightly closed.

Four hours later and a small crushed up banana received the same treatment from Dorothy. I spent over two hours coaxing and urging small amounts of banana through even more tightly clenched lips. Something was definitely very wrong. Dorothy wouldn't even accept a fruit flavoured drink, which normally she

92

tried to gulp down, if I'd let her. Also a slight tremor, which had started in her arms, had now spread to her lower body. I walked the dozen steps from the bedside to the telephone in the hall. The receptionist at the surgery knew of Dorothy's condition, being a regular patient of Dr. Morris. She put me through immediately saying his last patient was due to leave in a few minutes. The reassuring voice of Dr. Morris cut in, "I'll be with you both in approximately fifteen minutes".

The good doctor was true to his word but, even during those few minutes, Dorothy's condition had deteriorated considerably. I knew it was a second stroke, even before Dr. Morris confirmed it. After quickly ringing 999 for an ambulance, he returned to the bedside. Putting a hand on my shoulder, he said, with genuine empathy I'd become so accustomed to, "It's another severe stroke, Dorothy may not have the strength to withstand this one". He left and I didn't have long to wait for the ambulance. I could hear its sinister wail a mile away.

Following the ambulance for a short time I realised I couldn't exceed the speed limit: they could. The ambulance accelerated away leaving me wondering if Dorothy would be returned to me at "Horner Towers".

It was over eight weeks before she was discharged. The first week was spent in Intensive Care, followed by a spell in a High Dependency Unit. During the later weeks, a Registrar informed me that Dorothy could no longer swallow and required an operation for PEG to be inserted into her stomach. Before her discharge, I was given tuition on how to operate the feeding system which fed into her PEG. Not difficult of course, just a case of practice makes perfect.

Everything Dorothy needed to keep her alive went via the PEG system directly into the stomach. Her feed duration is ten hours for a thousand mls or one litre. I set the apparatus for a hundred mls an hour and it stops automatically when the litre is completed. The containers of liquid feed are supplied by Nutricia: they are delivered to my house directly and are on prescription.

93

All the vitamins from A to Z are included in the feed mix, along with multi fibres and enzymes.

Dorothy always enjoyed her meals but now each meal was tasteless to her. Her medication and water, to avoid dehydration, are sucked into a syringe and pumped via the PEG, directly into her tummy. Twice a week, I rotate the PEG through 360 degrees to avoid the thin pipe "jellifying" and subsequently "seizing up", inside the stomach.

I use distilled or boiled, cooled water to flush out the entire PEG regularly.

Also, and so very importantly, a "bubble" of water containing 5 mls of water needs to be checked weekly. This is done using a tiny syringe to withdraw the contents of the "bubble" If only 3 mls are shown to be inside the "bubble", 2 mls are added to make 5mls and returned back to the "bubble".

If, sometime in the future, you need to perform this not too complex PEG maintenance, take your time, there's no rush, but wash your hands thoroughly before commencing.

Dorothy had only been home for three or four days when I suspected she was in pain. She couldn't speak but she appeared to wince if I moved her right leg, which was necessary when pad changing. I asked Dr. Morris if he could examine Dorothy; the result of this was that he discovered a broken right hip. Where did this occur? During her stay in hospital, he thought. When? Within the last week, the Doctor considered. Dorothy was unable to complain about any pain. She also had a large bedsore on the base of her spine, and also on the heel of her right foot.

Back to hospital but, on this occasion, not to Intensive Care. A basic hip replacement operation was performed and Dorothy was back with me in ten days or so.

The bed sore, or pressure sore, as they are now commonly called, on Dorothy's heel was to take over twelve months to heal. A cast was made to avoid direct contact with the mattress. A wonderful idea, which worked.

A further few words about the PEG system. Don't, dear reader, be afraid of its maintenance procedure. Professional staff will help you through every small detail. Every three months the complete PEG is renewed. All you need to do is watch. Any queries? The truly helpful staff will demonstrate until you are confident in all aspects. In the unlikely event of something really important going wrong, you have an emergency telephone number to bring help very quickly to your loved one.

I consider the first stroke in 2006 to be the worse single event during Dorothy's period of Alzheimer's. Why? Because it took away every last vestige of freedom we both shared. All conversation and understanding - gone! Weekend trips to the coast and wheelchair walks along the promenade - gone! Monthly, week-long holidays at our daughters in London and the joy of seeing the grandchildren - gone! The cessation of the weekly walk around Hollingworth Lake - gone forever! Dorothy asking me hundreds of times a day, "Will I always have Alzheimer's"? In retrospect, these were, in an absurd sort of way, the "golden days" of this terrible affliction. Now, over two years since her second stroke, Dorothy lives her life, unaware that her family, and the true friends who visit her, love her dearly.

CHAPTER 23

DOROTHY SWALLOWS HER TONGUE

After her second stroke, Dorothy went through a calm period. The hip operation healed quickly and Doctor Morris agreed to prescribe a sleeping draught.

For two years I had noticed that during the night, when I came downstairs to check her, Dorothy was invariably awake. I'm a poor sleeper - I hardly ever manage much more than four hours sleep a night but I wanted Dorothy to sleep and wake up to a new day. It seemed inhuman to me that, apart from dozing on and off, she didn't have a regular long sleep. Doctor Morris is not a great believer in sleeping medication. He says that it loses its effectiveness after a period of time anyway. However, after pleading Dorothy's case that she deserved a period of being unconscious, he acquiesced.

"Temazepam" now helps Dorothy to drift off into a deep sleep. I still check how she is twice during the night and she is always sound asleep. Thank you Doctor Morris! I mix the "Temazepam" with Dorothy's other medication, topped up with cooled, boiled water, and insert via the PEG. By the time I've changed her pad, her eyelids are fluttering and two minutes later its "lights out".

I need to go out at certain times of the week or month. I do the weekly shop at Morrisons combined with filling up the car if the gauge is low or to the Health Centre to hand in Dorothy's prescription , collecting it two days later and waiting at the Pharmacy for the medication to be dispensed. Then, of course, there's my haircut every five or six weeks. So, I can't always be at Dorothy's side. In a perfect scenario I would be. Or should I have just written, in a perfect world, I would be?

My sons are both in full-time employment. They visit us regularly and if I visit friends or relatives at the weekend they ladysit their Mum.

On the afternoon that Dorothy swallowed her tongue, I hadn't been out of the house all day. I'd spent a large part of the morning sitting with her and just reminiscing about happier times.

Dorothy, possibly every three or four weeks or so, had what I called her "respiratory attack". I'd called out an ambulance when the first "attack" occurred but after several of these, I was confident enough to sit it out, as after ten to fifteen minutes, her laboured breathing would return to normal.

I'd drifted into the kitchen and started to prepare a pan of stew for tea. Every 5 or 6 minutes, I always check Dorothy to make sure she hasn't put too many fingers in her mouth and can't extract them. I'd checked out Dorothy maybe three minutes earlier when I heard a "throaty" noise from the sitting room. She'll have put four fingers into her mouth, I was thinking, as I left the kitchen. I was surprised when I saw that she didn't have any fingers in her mouth. But why was this terrible noise coming from her? I didn't think in terms of a stroke but, with every second that passed, the hideous noise increased in volume. I raised her from the pillow but this seemed to worsen the situation. Beads of sweat appeared on her forehead and there was a look of terror in her eyes. Good God! She's choking, she's fighting for her life! What do I do? Mouth to mouth resuscitation? Yes! Open her mouth and blow life giving air into her lungs. No! It's not working. She's going to die! God! After all we've been through together over these long years, I'm here and I can't help her.! Panic was beginning to set in. By this time, Dorothy was purple in the face when an inspired moment gave me hope. Footballers swallow their tongues. I'd seen it on televised matches. The medic runs out and withdraws the tongue with his fingers. Opening Dorothy's mouth, I realised her tongue was not in her mouth. Pushing my thumb and forefinger down her throat I immediately felt it. Way down her throat and as slippery as an

97

eel. Third attempt did it. I withdrew the tongue back into her mouth and the inhalation of air in dear Dorothy's lungs, was music to my ears. Oh joy! If I hadn't had heard her struggling for breath or if I'd been upstairs in a back bedroom or taking a shower, then Dorothy would have died.

The tears came five minutes later when I realised the enormity of what had almost happened.

Alzheimer's is a multi-faceted illness. Anything, yes anything, can happen at any moment. Carers beware!

CHAPTER 24

WASHING DOROTHY'S HAIR AND SOME CARERS TIPS

For decades, Dorothy visited a Ladies Hairdresser which was just around the corner. Every Saturday morning, rain or shine, she would walk the three hundred yards to "Pauline's" - and an excellent job Pauline made of her hair.

Towards the middle of stage two of the Alzheimer's, Dorothy became confused about finding the hairdresser's she'd frequented for 30 years, so I walked her round to "Pauline's" and Pauline rang me when she had finished ,to say that I could now escort my wife home.

Eventually, Pauline retired, so we needed to find a new hairdresser. "Blondes and Brunettes" situated locally in Chadderton fitted the bill adequately. Sue is a gifted hairdresser and so every fourth Tuesday- "pensioners' day" - Dorothy had a cut and blow. I'd opted for Dorothy's hairstyle to be a simple, low maintenance "bob", and it suited her really well. Even as Dorothy deteriorated and spent much of her waking hours in her wheelchair, Sue attended to her without any problems.

Unfortunately, the stroke in 2006 ended our happy association with Sue at "Blondes and Brunettes". I did ask Sue if she would continue with Dorothy's cut and blow at our home but it would have required Sue to do the cut and blow with Dorothy in a horizontal position in bed, but she declined and I really didn't blame her. Thank you Sue for all you did.

After a few weeks lying in bed 24/7, I realised that Dorothy's hair really did need washing and trimming. I telephoned several mobile hairdressers but because of Dorothy's disablement, they regretfully declined.

My daughters both live in faraway London and Dorothy's cut and wash was required right now or tomorrow. As it worked out, I'd decided, that Monday morning, that it was "now or never". Washing Dorothy's hair in the bath had not been a problem but I knew that in her present condition, it was going to be a major undertaking. This, the job that the professionals had refused, had become my responsibility! It wasn't just a matter of washing Dorothy's hair - she'd had it washed regularly in hospital - but the job also entailed cutting. Apart from some movement from her elbows up to her fingers, mainly in her right arm, Dorothy was otherwise totally paralysed. The job I was attempting was daunting, I knew that. How to start? Where to start? I decided to restore the fringe which was part of Dorothy's bob cut. Covering her eyes and removing the hair strands as I progressed, the fringe slowly took shape. On completing the fringe, I was amazed by the confidence which now filled me. Next, the back and sides of Dorothy's "locks" Log roll to the left, log roll to the right. Yes, it was taking shape. Eat your heart out Vidal Sassoon!

The shampooing and conditioning was "sleight of hand". Where that third hand came from I'll never know but suffice it to say, apart from having to change the saturated bottom sheet of the bed, the hair wash was completed, together with much rinsing, in about 40 minutes. I looked at the final result after finishing off with the hairdryer. Wow! Dorothy seemed to know that something different had happened that day. Beginner's luck!

Washing Dorothy's hair was far from easy, of course, but I managed reasonably well and Liz, my elder daughter, would assist, if she was visiting us for a few days. Over quite a span of time, Dorothy at least was better coiffured but single-handed it was, at best, a difficult undertaking.

Then, a minor miracle occurred. A long flat cardboard carton was delivered to the house. I hadn't ordered anything and it wasn't anywhere near our birthdays or Christmas. I could not describe the object which Liz had seen on the Internet and ordered for me to help with her Mum's hairdressing. Whoever thought up the idea of a triangular tray with a spout is a genius. Thank you genius, take a bow.

Avail yourself of one of these hair washing trays with a spout for bed use. Price - under £40 - and your loved one's shampoo day will never be a problem again!

As your loved one becomes incontinent, for less than a £1 you may purchase a key which fits all the disabled toilets in Britain: I'm not sure about the EU countries. Inside one of these toilets is sufficient space for a wheelchair and lots of manoeuvrability.

Dorothy, in her early days of Alzheimer's, would queue with the rest of the ladies at a Motorway Service toilet but, owning a disabled key avoids queuing up and can avoid "accidents" whilst having to wait in the queue. Always put a changing bag in the car, even on a short run. This could avoid a messy time when arriving home. Carry the quite large disabled toilet key with you at all times. It is no use arriving at an obscure disabled toilet, complete with your changing bag, having left the key on the kitchen table.

As a man, I found the job of putting on Dorothy's tights was quite difficult. The solution, as any lady would know is simple - merely concertina from top to toe and pull up the tights to the waist. Job done!

As your loved one becomes slower at using their knife and fork, cut everything up into quite small pieces, i.e., potatoes, meat, Yorkshire pudding (and dessert). This enables them to dispense completely with the knife and fork and use only the dessert spoon. Much quicker! Eventually, as in Dorothy's case, eating skills are lost completely. With a meal already in smaller pieces, you can feed your loved one, and eat yourself, without the hot meal rapidly becoming a cold one.

When taking a walk in the park or in a local beauty spot, a wheelchair is a "must-have" item. Your loved one can rest and relax as you "earn" your Carer's Allowance. Remember though that your Carer's Allowance will cease as you start on State Pension; unless State Pension is less than Carer's Allowance - very unlikely!! Secure your loved one around the waist, by tying them to the backrest of the wheelchair. Velcro tape can temporarily secure your loved one's feet to the footrest. Very important if they try to touch the ground as the wheelchair is in motion.

In the home, whilst in the early stage, mark each door with its name, e.g., Kitchen, Dining Room, Toilet, Lounge, Bathroom, etc. Big and Bold! This really works. But, because this is Alzheimer's I'm writing about, not indefinitely.

If, like myself, you are the main, full-time Carer, prepare all meals and cups of tea or coffee. Please do not expose your loved one to the risk of scalds and burns. In the bathroom, an Alzheimer's sufferer can easily stand touching the radiator or towel warmer and burn their body. Just have these adjustable items on warm, not hot. Supervise all baths or showers. Most safety first ideas are basic, sound common sense. Hold their hand crossing all roads. Go first where steps are concerned and help your loved one down. Treat everything as a possible hazard. - not to us maybe but to an Alzheimer's victim, an accident waiting to happen.

Perhaps dear reader you would consider a stair lift to transfer your loved one from ground to first floor and vice versa. I didn't bother with this for Dorothy but I wish I had. Much safer either up or down the stairs. Some local councils will supply a stair lift free. If not and you decide on one, buy a second hand model and save lots of precious cash.

As soon as Dorothy became bedridden, I decided to have a water meter fitted. I have a daily shower, not a daily bath and save lots of water that way. It's free to have one fitted and if, after twelve months, you consider it to be dearer than water rates, you can have it removed free of charge. My water rates for a year were £568 (including sewage charges); the charge for twelve months, in my case, is approximately £185 - again, this includes the sewage cleansing charges.

When shopping, consider "own brands" . I know for certain Morrison's own brand baked beans are canned by HP. They're delicious and are half the price of Heinz baked beans. Try various "own brands" and save money.

Buy your gas and electricity from the same energy company. Pay monthly on direct debit and save approximately 9% on the deal. Sign up to a long-term agreement and your prices will be frozen during that term.

When driving, press down on the "gas pedal" gently and get into top gear as soon as possible. Drive at only at 40 or 50 mph in a 40 or 50 mph zone. Never exceed 70 mph on the Motorways. Exceed these speeds and you could risk a fine. Also drive faster than the legal limits and you're the car in front of mine at the next red traffic light!! Drive sensibly and save 12% on your fuel bills.

Using your free travel pass is a good idea. Not so good, if your loved one is wheelchair-bound, as Dorothy was for several years. Don't forget to apply for 25% off your Council Tax bill if there's only two of you living at the same address.

Placing security chains on the front and bedroom doors is a must, once your loved one has started to wander. These are easy to purchase at most supermarkets or B&Q. Fitting is quite basic DIY, but you lady Carers can always ask for help from a relative or family friend. Fit the security chains within a couple of inches or so of the top of each door. This will render the task of undoing the chain by an Alzheimer's sufferer almost impossible. Before I fitted a security chain to the bedroom door, there could have been a major accident. At 3.00 a.m. one morning Dorothy, whilst I was sleeping, opened the bedroom door and fell downstairs in total darkness. Just cuts and bruises ensued but it could have been broken bones! I fitted a security chain that afternoon.

For several years, Dorothy stood by the kitchen door and watched me prepare cooked meals. She enjoyed watching and chatting as I worked. I resisted the temptation of allowing her to assist. Alzheimer's sufferers have forgotten all about danger. Even cutting up carrots can lead to a deep cut and boiling pans are lethal.

Even if, like Dorothy, your loved one is immobile in bed 24/7 and PEG fed, they really appreciate, several times a day, a drop of water on their lips and inside the mouth. This can be achieved easily by using a short stick with a circular piece of sponge-like substance attached to one end. I first saw these in use in hospital, and chemists and medical suppliers stock them in packs of ten. I call them "lollipops".

They are a must, especially during the summer but after a night's sleep your loved one's mouth must be crying out for water!

I've mentioned elsewhere in these chapters, the advantage of an hydraulic chair for use in the bath. An absolute must when our loved ones lose their sense of balance and the ability to climb in and out of the bath.

Baby wipes are necessary for cleaning up after incontinence attacks, when a loved one is finally bedridden. Morrison's sell four packs for £3. Easily as good as more expensive wipes which cost double the price.

Buy Sanex shower cream when it is on offer at half-price. A squirt in the morning bath water makes for healthier skin. Stock up and keep them in a box under the bed, for easy access, along with syringes, medications and skin creams.

Changing an incontinence pad is easier with practice, of course. The pads supplied on the NHS on prescription could be larger, but "mustn't look a gift horse in the mouth". Fitting one by yourself is a matter of "log roll" to the left, then to the right. Centralise the pad as near as possible and finish off by pulling up "the slack" towards your loved one's back. Hold the pad in place with a pair of muslin knickers.

Finally, just a brief resume of helpful hints. Do not, I repeat do not, allow the ostracism of neighbours and ex-friends towards you and your loved one, affect you in any way, shape or form! Concentrate your thoughts on good neighbours, good friends, your family and most of all, your loved one!!

CHAPTER 25

LEARN TO LOVE WHAT WE HAVE, NOT WHAT WE WANT

What would you do dear reader, with the money, if you won millions of pounds on "Lotto" or "Euromillions? Pay off the mortgage, buy a mansion on Mayfair, the latest 200 mph Ferrari, a holiday villa in the south of France or even a small island in the Caribbean? All these things would be possible if you had a massive win! And Good Luck to you too. We all have an equal chance every week, for a £1 or £2 ticket to live the dream. The odds of landing the jackpot are enormous but, "You have to be in it, to win it".

So what would I do if I won say, £2 million? I haven't a great need of luxury items, at nearing 75 years of age. I love my eight-years-old, short wheelbase RAV 4, but for the summer, I might buy the basic, two-seater Morgan sports car at £31,500. Most of the £2 million, I would give to worthy causes, (definitely the Alzheimer's Society), and to family and friends. I'm one of those people who prefer to give someone a present in preference to receiving one.

I won £90 on the Lottery a few weeks ago. That's the most money I have won, at any time in my life. I like the fact that for every £1 spent on the Lottery, fifty pence goes to very worthy causes. When I had my "big win", I didn't rush off to order my Morgan (they take months to build), because obviously £90 is only capable of buying a petrol fill up at Morrisons and maybe the weekly shop.

When I was demobilised from HM Forces, after completing my two years National Service, in the 1950s, I had one shilling, (five pence) to my name. It seemed a daunting task to save the deposit money for a little terraced house, but like all the young people of that era, we did it. There is a sense of achievement as the final few pounds are saved.

If I won the £2 million, which would benefit many people, I'd have 2,000 copies of "WIAHA?" delivered to my local Morrisons and give every shopper I saw, a free copy.

But in the real world, not the world of "if only", we all know that £10 is the sum of money we are most likely to win! My Morgan sports car, with its wooden chassis, would look lovely on my driveway but my 8 years old RAV 4 (SWB) is a joy to drive and I can only drive one car at a time.

Loving the things we have, and not what we want, is easy, when we consider that we haven't any alternative. What we actually own is a world away from an object of desire which, unless we defeat the odds of 14 million to one, we'll never be able to afford.

"Be careful what you wish for, you just might get it!" I wonder who first said that well-coined phrase? "If wishes were horses, then beggars would ride". That phrase is possibly centuries old. An adage passed down through the ages.

To live a decent, industrious life, following the cardinal virtues, the most important moral qualities being: justice, prudence, temperance and fortitude, are paramount for a happy, contented life.

We, dear Carers, need fortitude more than most people, as we care for our loved ones. Calm and patient courage in trouble or pain. Yes, that's exactly what is required of an Alzheimer Carer!

For the last nineteen years, as a Carer, I've always appreciated what I have. I still have Dorothy, I have my family and friends - things that money can't ever buy!

I often wonder if our feathered friends, the birds, suffer stress. They know nothing about religion, avarice, drugs, alcohol or dying. They know about self-preservation and could suffer during a harsh winter but, by and large, they seem happy with their little lives.

I'm sorry that Dorothy and I can no longer travel. We loved travelling abroad. In 1994, 1995, 1996, 1997, and 1998 we travelled widely, but not anymore. I have the photographs and memories to remind me. Memories are experiences of one's life. They can never be taken away!

CHAPTER 26

"ONE MEATBALL WITHOUT NO GRAVY"

Hands up dear readers, if you've ever sang along, when you've heard this Tune on the radio. It's very "catchy".

"One meatball, without no gravy!
One meatball, without no gravy!
One meatball, without no gravy!
You get no bread with one meatball!"

Another song, written possibly during the United States depression years of post 1929 is, "Brother can you spare a dime?" Not so "catchy" as "One meatball" but a song of that era.

So why am I writing about USA depression music? And what has this got to do with the price of sprouts? Nothing!

However, somewhere in North London, on Tuesday mornings, if you pass a certain building, you can hear the refrain of "one meatball" and other favourite songs for sing-alongs.

My elder daughter, Liz, has recently started voluntary work on Tuesday mornings at a "Singing for the Brain "session. It's run by the Alzheimer's Society. Both Liz and my younger daughter, Dee, have supported the Alzheimer's Society throughout the years. They buy Alzheimer's Society Christmas cards every year which, along with thousands of others, raises vital funds. Raffles also raise lots of lovely cash.

Liz attends this centre and helps people with dementia pass a pleasant morning. I'm quite sure there is more to the morning than just singing – Being together having teas and coffees afterwards in a supportive environment.

In most areas throughout the UK there are Alzheimer's Centres. The early onset centres are the easiest and cheapest to run because they require fewer staff.

I have mentioned the Carisbrooke Centre already in this book. This centre caters only for stage one Alzheimer's. Just like many others, sixty years of age is the cut off age. Lack of resources is the reason that this wonderful centre has to ration its usage. Dorothy enjoyed every minute at the Carisbrooke Centre and would have loved to have carried on there, way beyond sixty.

Perhaps some time in the future when Alzheimer's has better funding from the Government, the centres will be able to welcome our loved ones way beyond the age of only sixty!

Now then, back to that song. I wonder if there's a second verse? How about:

"One meatball, it looks quite greasy!
One meatball, it is quite greasy!
One meatball, why is it greasy?
You won't get fat on one meatball!"

CHAPTER 27

THE FEAR WE ALL DREAD: PNEUMONIA

On Sunday, 2 September 2012, I became increasingly alarmed as the morning progressed. Dorothy was running a temperature and a cough was developing. Her breathing was wheezy and rattling. After her bed bath, she is normally wide eyed and turning her head, but not this Sunday morning. She just lay there, eyes closed.

Through the experience of assessing Dorothy every day since her first stroke left her bedridden, I knew the perils of pneumonia. She had had a few chest infections, which Doctor Morris had treated quickly. But that was then, and this was now.

My gut feeling told me that today was different. I had this ominous sense of foreboding. Not a premonition, per se, but because it was Sunday, I couldn't telephone the Health Centre for Doctor Morris to visit and tell me, in his cheerful, confident voice, that all was well (or not).

The morning became afternoon and Dorothy started to moan, possibly because of the pain. At about 4.00 p.m. I knew that I needed the Locum to examine her and prescribe medication.

I had never called out the Locum before and initially wondered what the procedure was. At the Health Centre, quite obviously they realise people need a doctor "out of hours". The information on the recorded message gave this vital telephone number. The person at the end of the line required lots of information about Dorothy before she set the wheels in motion. The Locum is hard pressed to visit all the sick people in the area and the telephone receptionist has the last word - she prioritises. I was able to convince her that Dorothy was very ill and needed medication. I think that possibly what swayed the matter in my favour was the fact that I said, that if the Locum was too busy, I would call out the paramedics.

Eventually, at 6.30 p.m., the Locum arrived and within a couple of minutes diagnosed pneumonia He was thorough and definite. The word "pneumonia" seemed to echo around Dorothy's bedroom and bounce around my head. Thinking that Dorothy could hear and understand what he was saying, the Doctor drew me into the adjacent hallway. "People like your wife", he said softly, "can die very easily with double bronchial pneumonia". I didn't say that I was already aware of this fact but thanked him for the prescription.

Not realising that a list of chemist shops, open until very late at the weekends, is on display at my local chemist, I telephoned North Manchester General Hospital for information. The telephone receptionist obviously wasn't aware of this either and just said that she couldn't help me on this matter.

Lou and Sue, two of Dorothy's nurses, arrived about 7.00 p.m. and Lou telephoned her supervisor for information on chemists which were open. The supervisor rang back within minutes to say that on the south side of Manchester, Lloyd's Pharmacy on Wilmslow Road, was open until 10.30 p.m. Thankfully, I arrived back home from my 16 miles round trip by 8.00 p.m. to start Dorothy on the life-saving antibiotic medication.

Antibiotic medicine is a wonderful cure, which has been prescribed by doctors for many years. It must have cured millions of people worldwide but it is not infallible and cannot always cure the chronically ill, especially Alzheimer's sufferers, paralysed in bed. The dosage was for three 10 mls per 24 hours. Dorothy, via her feeding PEG had her first 10 mls by 8.00 p.m. I was glad to have the antibiotics with which to fight the pneumonia on the Sunday evening and not to have Dorothy wait until the following day when I knew that, after informing the Health Centre of her condition, Doctor Morris would visit to examine his patient.

I had already decided by 11.30 p.m. on that Sunday, that I would stay with Dorothy ready to administer the second dose of

112

antibiotics at 4.00 a.m. on Monday morning. She was restless, even with the sleeping medicine she has at 11.00 p.m. every night. She was running a massively high temperature and moaning in obvious pain and I was tempted to telephone 999 for an ambulance but I drew back from the scenario of Dorothy back in hospital again. My confidence shattered by various experiences at Crumpsall Hospital and the broken hip, I decided her recovery was better left in the hands of Doctor Morris and me, as Dorothy's long-term Carer and devoted husband.

Wiping Dorothy's forehead in the early hours of Monday morning, I became aware of a pinkish coloured "gunge" emanating from the corner of her mouth. I wiped it up with a single piece of kitchen roll but, immediately, more "gunge" appeared. It seemed to be endless. The flow of this disgusting-looking discharge lasted until just before 4.00 a.m.- then it stopped. I'd used up a complete kitchen roll and filled the pedal bin. I emptied the pedal bin into the wheelie bin and washed my hands. Time for the second dose of antibiotics.

When Doctor Morris arrived after his morning surgery, he examined Dorothy thoroughly, confirming that it was, indeed, double pneumonia, the most deadly type. He asked me if I'd prefer Dorothy to be in hospital. I declined for the reasons I've already given and he nodded in agreement.

Dr Morris, who had seen every facet of treating Dorothy for Alzheimer's during the last nineteen years, had already, on a previous occasion when Dorothy had bronchitis, gently informed me that the worst could occur. He reminded me again of the possible consequences, especially with bronchial pneumonia. He prescribed another antibiotic medicine to be taken along with the one the Locum had prescribed. This I liked! Two antibiotics, working in unison, to beat Dorothy's pneumonia!

I cannot speak too highly of Doctor Morris during the four weeks before Dorothy's lungs were clear of fluid. He visited twice a week and telephoned me in between visits to check on her progress. He really is a dedicated doctor and a credit to his indispensible profession.

The antibiotics took their time to do their work and Doctor Morris prescribed another ten days course after the initial ten days had passed.

About two weeks into the pneumonia, I was sitting with Dorothy . The pain in her chest must have been intense, which I gauged by her frequent moans. I had her bed adjusted so that she was lying at an angle of 45 degrees but on this occasion her coughing bout had lasted for twenty minutes and the veins on her forehead stood out prominently. "How can I help you sweetheart?" I said out loud in near desperation. Then, as though inspired, I had an idea. Taking one of Dorothy's large syringes, I decided that I must try something to help her. Using the syringe systematically, I started to "suck" a horrible yellowish/green, sticky bile from her mouth and throat. After about half an hour, I had removed about a quarter of a pint of this hideous substance. Magically, the coughing stopped and within minutes of administering her sleeping medicine, Dorothy was in the "land of nod".

Doctor Morris visited on Friday, 28 September, at 9.00 a.m. whilst the nurses were still "finishing off" Dorothy's toiletry. I introduced him to Lou and Sue - "This is Doctor Morris, the best doctor in the world". He replied by saying, "I wouldn't be here now, but for this man's caring, Dorothy would have been dead years ago". Thank you so much for saying that about me Doctor Morris. I've never felt more proud in all my life!

On Sunday, 30 September, I looked into Dorothy's face as I held her hand. The crisis was over - she had come through an attack of pneumonia that a fully healthy person would have struggled against. Well done, Dorothy! Your "time" has not yet come.

I looked at my grey face in the mirror, which matched my grey hair. I felt exhausted but triumphant.

CHAPTER 28

"WHAT A DIFFERENCE ONE DAY CAN MAKE"

I thought long and hard before deciding to write this chapter. Over the years, since 1980, good, decent, down-to-earth people, have asked me if the events of August 1980 had such a devastating effect on Dorothy that, years later, in 1994 (or most likely the year before) she contracted Alzheimer's. My thoughts on what occurred on Tuesday, 19 August 1980, are that my younger daughter's accident on that day, did not cause Dorothy's Alzheimer's. End of!

Thirty-two years ago, Dorothy and I were forty-two and our younger daughter, Dee, was thirteen. She had passed through the Brownies and into the Girl Guides. Saturday, 16 August was to be an exciting day for Dee. She and the Girl Guides were off for a week of camping at a local beauty spot - Ashworth Valley - which is situated between Rochdale and Bury. I was just about to enter my greenhouse as Dee came bounding down the garden to give me a kiss and say bye-bye. I had two crisp one-pound notes in my back pocket which I gave to her. "Be careful, don't do anything silly", I remember saying as we hugged. Little did I know then, that it would be three months before Dee slept in her own bed again.

I had my car loaded with garden waste and set off for the local "dump". Driving past St. Chad's Church, I noticed a mini-coach full of girl guides and the Guide Captain standing on the pavement, adjacent to it. Possibly waiting for a late comer, I mused as I indicated to turn right.

That summer of 1980 had not been a particularly good one, but better by far than this summer of 2012 and last year, 2011. On my return journey I noticed that the coach had left. I hoped that the weather would be sunny and dry during the camping week.

Fast forward exactly 72 hours to Tuesday, 19 August 1980. Why is it that I have instant recall of everything that happened that day, complete with coloured pictures? Thirty-two years on, I can see myself potting the black ball into the green corner pocket, to win a "black-ball" game of snooker. Pleased with my win, against a better player, I took the lift down from the Games Room on the top floor to the first floor of the telephone exchange. Dinner break over, soon be 4.00 p.m. and hometime.

Pete Buckley was obviously waiting for me to return from the mid-day break. He was sitting on my chair at my workbench. Seeing me approaching, he came towards me and informed me that I'd received two telephone calls during my absence; one from my wife, the second from Steve, my younger son, who had called from home. Both messages were the same: to ring back ASAP.

I rang Dorothy first. The office junior said that she'd had to go home. This made sense when I rang Steve back. He said Dee had fallen at the camp and broken her ankle.

During the summer, I used a push bike as my means of transport, I rode home flat out, sweat pouring from every pore.

Dorothy was already home and a man called Malc, who was the husband of one of the guide leaders, had dropped in. He said that Dee had only broken her ankle. I wasn't too sure that that was 100% correct.

I took a quick shower and backed the car out of the garage. After a cup of coffee, I led the way to Bury General Hospital, Malc following. Bury is about ten or eleven miles away and I easily picked up the signs for the hospital. Parking was free in those days - how times change! I took Dorothy's hand and we walked to the A & E entrance. I'd had an ominous feeling since coming off the M66: now my heart leapt into my mouth as I saw two police cars parked close to the A & E Department. I sensed that they were there because of Dee's "broken ankle". Within the next two

117

minutes every parent's worst nightmare was about to become reality.

Spotting a Sister, I said our daughter was the Girl Guide who had had an accident. She took us into a cubicle where Dee was. The absolute horror and shock of seeing our beautiful daughter, the baby of the family, with such terrible injuries almost caused me to faint. I pulled myself together with great difficulty and knew that, more than at any time of our married life together, Dorothy needed my mental strength and support. She looked ghastly, tears rolling down her cheeks. I wanted to shout out, "Let's wake up right now Dorothy, I can't bear this nightmare". But the deadly truth had already had its impact on me minutes before. Dee was very seriously injured and only the skill of the doctors, surgeons and Intensive Care staff could save her life!

Dee's head appeared to be enlarging before my eyes but the injury I could not take my eyes off was her lower lip, which was almost hanging off. (As recently as 29 September 2012, Dee had an operation to improve the appearance of her lower lip - 32 years and 41 days after the fall! Dental work has been ongoing since 1980!)

Dorothy and I were asked to say goodbye to Dee, in case she didn't make it through the next few hours and the operation was about to commence. It was surreal: I felt like death.

We left Bury about 5.00 p.m. I rang the hospital at about 7.00 p.m. but Dee was still in Theatre and constant calls could tell me nothing. Eventually, at 10.30 p.m., I was informed that Dee was out of Theatre and in Intensive Care. The operation had gone well! Every hour of that sleepless night, I rang Intensive Care. "As well as can be expected" was all the Sister would tell me.

I turned in for work next morning and was immediately granted a week's compassionate leave. The news of the brave little Girl Guide falling 50 feet at Ashworth Valley had been on the radio, television news and in the Manchester Evening News.

I was back at the Intensive Care Unit by 11.00 a.m. Dee was sleeping. Her head was completely swathed in bandages, only her eyes visible. A tube led from her mouth for feeding purposes. Dee's left thigh bone (femur) was broken in several places and was raised about two feet high and held on traction. Apart from internal injuries most of the impact of the fall had caused a skull fracture, broken jaws, smashed teeth, perforated eardrums, where the jaws had been driven upwards and the almost complete severance of the lower lip.

I was informed that the next 48 hours were crucial. I sat holding Dee's hand for the next hour until the staff said they needed to change some dressings. Also, a police officer was waiting to see me in the Sister's office.

I was still in a state of shock after my daughter's accident but what the officer told me in the following ten minutes, made me feel sick to my stomach. Apparently, a couple walking on the other side of the river to where Dee fell, had seen her fall. The man said to his wife that he was going to the girl's aid. She reminded him that he had health issues and must not try to negotiate such a tricky descent. Heated words were exchanged but this brave Polish gentleman was adamant and his wife proceeded on her way home whilst he went to help Dee. Hours later at about 9.30 p.m. his wife telephoned Bury General Hospital to ask to speak to her husband, whom she thought must have travelled there in the ambulance. An attentive Police Officer "picked up" on the telephone conversation and took the receiver. The Polish gentleman wasn't at home, nor was he at the hospital. The Officer rang his Inspector who told him to take flood lighting equipment and search the area where Dee had fallen. An hour later, the courageous Polish gentleman was found. He had been dead for several hours as the result of a heart attack. This tragic story also appeared in daily newspapers - and on television news.

The Police Officer was speaking to me about this terrible event but, suddenly, my hearing "switched off". His mouth was opening and closing but all I could hear was the voice in my brain screaming, "Dee is not certain to survive and now a brave man, who had gone to help her, was dead."

119

I sent flowers and a letter to the Polish lady, expressing our condolences and how public-spirited and brave her husband had been but, he was gone forever, and she didn't reply to me. I can't blame her.

During the next few days I was able to piece together what had happened on the morning of Tuesday, 19 August 1980. The Guide Captain had assembled her girls and said, "Off you go girls, be back for dinner at 1.00 p.m." One of the girls asked, "Can we go anywhere in the Valley, Captain?" "Yes, you can" she replied, "as long as you're back here for 1.00 p.m." That was a massive error of judgement on her part. The other side of the river (more of a narrow stream) rose to a high escarpment, with a narrow path along the edge and no safety fence. The Guide Captain should have reconnoitred the Valley. If she had done so, then the escarpment side surely would have been made "out of bounds". Dee set out that morning with two other girls to explore the Valley. They had full permission to roam anywhere they wished.

At approximately 12.10 p.m. Dee was leading the way along this narrow path, which had now risen to 50 feet above the river. Suddenly, after having absorbed much rain that summer, the path gave way and Dee plummeted down onto the rocks, and ended up half submerged in the river below. A massive accident had just occurred. The rest, as they say, is now history.

On 4 September, sixteen days after the accident, I received a morning call at work from an Intensive Care Sister. Dee had just had a massive haemorrhage from her left ear and Dorothy and I were required immediately at the hospital. On the way to Bury, Dorothy and I did not exchange one word. I couldn't have spoken anyhow; the lump in my throat felt as large as an apple. I felt for poor Dorothy - she would be feeling just as wretched as I did.

Mr John Bradley, the Surgeon, was waiting for our arrival at Dee's bedside. Taking us into the Sister's Office, he explained what had occurred during the night. Blood had accumulated in Dee's head until it reached a high pressure and haemorrhaged from her ear. He stated categorically that an operation had to be performed to save Dee's life. The odds of success were evens! There are two arteries supplying blood to the brain, situated on either side of the neck. Mr. Bradley was to "tie back" Dee's left side artery.

Hours later, Dee was back in Intensive Care. She had come through the operation. Well done Dee, well done Mr. Bradley! Dee would have to manage with a single main artery to the brain. The scar initially was grotesque but has faded reasonably well over the years. The loss of many teeth and gum and root injuries have caused many, many visits to the Dental Hospital and dentists, over the ensuing decades.

In November 1980, Dee was discharged from Bury Hospital, albeit on crutches and wearing a calliper on her left leg from ankle to hip. There were to be years of out-patient visits stretching into the future but our little heroine had, after three months in hospital, survived!

Three years later, Dee and I were attending the Out-patients Department at Bury General Hospital. Her name was called and she went in to see the Orthopaedic Specialist by herself. Being now sixteen she had recently started seeing the Femur Specialist alone. I noticed a paramedic had stood up as Dee's name was called. Sauntering across to me he asked if the young girl whose name had just been called was Diane Horner. "Yes", I replied, "she's my daughter". The paramedic explained to me that he had been on duty on 19 August 1980 with a newly-qualified female paramedic, then just 23 years of age. They were called to Ashworth Valley where a Girl Guide had fallen many feet onto rocks. His young colleague abseiled down to where Dee lay. From the other side of the river a youth had seen Dee fall and had gone to assist her. Not knowing any first-aid whatsoever, he cradled Dee's head on his lap. The paramedic arrived at the scene of the accident just in time to save Dee's life. She was choking on blood that was literally drowning her. Within seconds, the paramedic had Dee in the recovery position, clearing the throat, lungs, and airways. Dee's young life had been saved, followed a second and third time by the skills of Mr. Bradley, Master Surgeon!

Just as the burly paramedic had finished explaining to me what had transpired that day, his slim colleague came across to him carrying two coffees. He grinned at me and said that he knew the date of Dee's accident because, "She" - he gestured towards the young woman, "received a Commendation for Bravery and saving an accident victim's life". My throat and mouth were dry, but I hugged and thanked this lovely paramedic, whom seconds before I had never met and three minutes before had had no idea that Dee almost died at the scene. This young paramedic had received a medal of commendation but she merely smiled and said, "I was just doing my job". Thirty-two years after that day, Dee and the rest of my family are still thanking you for your courage and expertise!

The cost of that week's camping for Dee was £14.00, £3.00 of which was personal insurance. Dorothy and I were so relieved that Dee had survived a life-threatening accident that it was not our intention to claim on the insurance. We were persuaded to take the case to the Crown Court with a compensation figure of £15,000. It was 1983 and settlements of six figures for injuries, were still many years away. The compensation figure of £15,000 was towards ongoing dental work for the replacement of teeth removed because of smashed jaws and splintered teeth. It was not a claim of people affected by avarice.

The case took seven years to eventually be heard at Court, at a cost to Dorothy and I of £8,000. Dee was assured by our Solicitors of a certain win. The process of litigation would have been, after winning the lawsuit, the refunding of our £8,000. We lost the lawsuit! The verdict went against Dee. Unbelievable! We were advised to appeal but years of mental anguish after the accident, regular out patient treatment, dental repair work and the pending and ever ongoing court case, had rendered us totally, mentally and physically exhausted. We did not appeal against the verdict! It was only money anyhow!

So, did the events leading to years of heartache and trauma cause Dorothy to become an Alzheimer victim? Many would say that the jury is still out. I am saying that Dee's accident and all the ensuing years of anguish had nothing to do with it! Alzheimer's is absolutely random.

Dee is now 46. She is the mother of two lovely children - Jakson, aged 15, and Saffron, aged 12. Dorothy and I have been blessed by the absolute pride and pleasure these wonderful grandchildren have given to us.

None of us will ever forget those dark days of 1980 but, as Dorothy used to say, "You've got to rise above it!"

CHAPTER 29

THE TERRIBLE TRUTH ABOUT ASHWORTH VALLEY

Please excuse me, dear readers, for adding to my previous chapter on the perils of Ashworth Valley. If I can make only one person aware of the "Valley of Death" then I shall be justified in penning this warning.

Prior to Dee's case being heard at the Manchester Crown Court, Dorothy and I were required, along with a civil engineer, our Solicitor and a photographer, to take measurements and photographs of the place where she fell. The two guides who were with Dee on the 19th August 1980, showed us the exact spot. On a danger score out of ten, this path, with the precipice on the left and the path eleven inches wide, would score a resounding ten.

Our Solicitor, that day, was of the opinion that the path, meandering upwards for fifty feet, was on private land. And yet there was no fence in place to prevent trespassers proceeding. Nor was there a "Keep out, Dangerous!" sign.

In the 32 years since our daughter's near-fatal fall, I have learned a lot about the dangers of Ashworth Valley: accidents along this path, some involving mounted horse riders, well before 1980, had occurred regularly. There have been several accidents since 1980. In 1995, a young boy scout, aged just 14, fell from this hideous path. This happened in the era of the mobile telephone and an ambulance was called very quickly but the staff at Bury General Hospital were unable to save Paul. A fractured skull was the cause of his death. Months later, Paul's father, whom everyone thought was "getting over" the death of his son, came out of a local public house where he had shared a few pints with friends, proceeded to his home and took his own life.

As I stood on the very same spot from which Dee plummeted, I felt the hairs on the back of my neck standing up. Hardly daring to breathe, I looked down the fifty feet to where the photographer stood with his camera. How could anyone survive a fall like that?

Over many years there have been several fatalities in Ashworth Valley: possibly as many as six or seven, together with the deaths of horses and dogs.

In the interests and safety of everyone in the future who will wish to explore this area of local beauty, I would say to the owner of the land where the path rises from river level to fifty feet, and to the local council, who must hold some sway, isolate this precarious area by erecting high railings so that never again, will good people suffer pain and even worse!

CHAPTER 30

A SATURDAY WITH DOROTHY: PRE ALZHEIMER'S

Like all of us, Dorothy enjoyed her weekends. This chapter tells us a little bit about how she spent her leisure time on a Saturday: baking and delivering.

Before Alzheimer's reared its ugly head, Dorothy would take alternate weekends with me for "a cuppa in bed". She made a fantastic cup of tea, far better than mine, or anyone else's.

After the breakfast pots were washed and put away, Dorothy would start her baking, prior to walking round to Pauline's, the hairdressers. She would bake all sorts of buns, cakes and tarts. The delicious aroma of baking emanated from "Horner Towers" and drifted along Hawthorn Road. I've been cleaning my car on the driveway and heard local people remark, "Dorothy's baking her usual Saturday batch of buns and tarts". I would grin to myself knowing that the Saturday batch of buns, tarts, cakes and apple pies would last us well into the following week.

After Dorothy's weekly visit to Pauline's, the hairdresser, she would start filling brown paper bags with "goodies" and load them into an old wicker-type shopping basket. Then, after our mid-day meal, she would set out on foot and deliver the paper bags to the old and sick people in the immediate vicinity. Race or creed did not enter into this wonderfully kind gesture. That is how Dorothy was!

Now? She lies paralysed and mute in our sitting room. Her kindness to older, sick people, is very strong still in my memory. Most of these older, sick people have now passed away. But Dorothy gave them this unique feeling on Saturday afternoons sometimes stretching into years! I can only imagine that unique

126

feeling, that a younger, busy person had taken the trouble to do something for them.

The years have slid by. Dorothy's bounding good health is now history. She is now much, much worse than the old, sick people to whom she delivered her delicious confectionery.

I'm so proud of what you did on Saturday afternoons Dorothy. All those people accepting the brown paper bags from you are gone or have now forgotten. You can't remember any of those days but I can!

With tears in my eyes, I bring to a close this short chapter. If I never write this again, I write it now. "You don't deserve what has happened to you Sweetheart, so sleep tight Kindheart, your Angel teddy is watching over you."

CHAPTER 31

"PEOPLE MAY FORGET WHAT WE DID OR SAID, BUT THEY WILL NEVER FORGET HOW WE MADE THEM FEEL"

The title of this chapter goes way beyond the profound. Read the title at least five or six times and the intensity of the words will jump off the page at you. The words will hold you transfixed.

It could be you, or I, dear reader, to whom the title alludes. It could be just about anyone living or dead but think of your loved one, as I am thinking, as I write, about Dorothy and the long ago past and all the yesterdays which constitute our lives together.

We may recall vividly, in Technicolor , some wonderful occasion or event from twenty years ago, or we may have forgotten what the occasion was but we are in thrall still, because of how we felt. The loved one made the event or day magical and the feelings will come back to us again and again - maybe even to haunt us.

It is almost as though Dorothy is speaking again, after all these years, to false friends and is saying, "You may have forgotten that I was once your friend but you will never forget how having me as a friend, made you feel". Rest assured, all you Alzheimer victims around the world that we, your carers, will never forget your life and the things you did before that thief of time, Alzheimer's, uninvited, came along and destroyed your future!

I recall saying to a neighbour from across the road who hadn't visited Dorothy in almost four years, that Dorothy and I would have visited them if they had had Alzheimer's. "I know you would" she mumbled but she has not been back! Stigma sticks!

Approaching, or beyond, what is now termed as elderly (65-75 years), most of our lives are in the past. Very often it's the memories and the feelings, derived from the past, which make us feel the nostalgia which can, so often, be bitter-sweet. Memories are good! Without them we wouldn't have a life to look back on. An Alzheimer victim, as we all know, once the illness is well advanced, has lost all memory and feelings of the past.

"Will I always have Alzheimer's?", the title of this book, harks back to the period when Dorothy asked me that question hundreds of times a day. Oh! For her to ask me that question now, just once more!

Last Sunday, 25 November 2012, I drove the 480 miles to London and back to deliver Christmas and birthday presents to my married daughters and my grandchildren. The nostalgia during that day was almost overpowering. For over 20 years, Dorothy sat by my side counting the Eddie Stobart lorries and listening to our beloved CDs. I counted 28 Eddie Stobart lorries on the way there and back, but I couldn't listen to any of the "sad songs". Feelings, eh!

CHAPTER 32

"CHANGING OUR CAR"

As Dorothy's mobility decreased, I decided to change our ten-years-old Nissan. It was during 2004 and there was a plethora of decent cars from which to choose. We liked the looks of the Mini and decided to take one for a test drive, which was totally satisfactory, and I decided this was the car for us: wide opening doors and plenty of space in the back for the wheelchair.

The saleslady offered me a good part-exchange price and I was about to shake hands on the deal when I suddenly thought of something important. "May I have another quick inspection of the rear compartment?" I asked. The saleslady raised the single lifting door and I looked upon the pristine, spacious area. "Where is the spare wheel kept?" I asked. "There isn't a spare wheel", she answered, Minis have "run-flat-tyres". I asked what these were exactly and she replied that segments of hard rubber running width-ways across the tyre every few inches stopped the wheel ever touching the road in the event of deflation.

All well and good, I thought, but when she informed me that 40 mph was the speed limit, I immediately realised that a puncture would require me to leave the motorway, as 40 mph is an unsafe speed to drive at on the motorways.

I've always owned cars with a spare wheel. For over 50 years every car had a full-sized spare. Some car manufacturers provide a "get-you-home", which is extremely narrow and could alter the geometry of the steering, if used as a front wheel spare.

I declined to buy a Mini for the reasons given. If everyone about to purchase a new car with a "pram wheel" spare declined, the car makers would very soon have a rethink and revert back to the "time-tested full-size-spare". Some car makers don't even supply a "pram wheel". They supply a puncture aerosol to repair the puncture via the air valve. Useless if the tyre damage is on the tyre wall!

So Dorothy and I drove from the BMW Mini Showroom, a few miles further on, to a Toyota Showroom. There, the first car I test drove was a "Celica". A fabulous coupe which was a joy to drive. Arriving back at the showroom, I very quickly realised the car was so low that I could not pull Dorothy from it. I needed the help of the car salesman and even then it was difficult! I rapidly tried two more cars but they didn't impress me. Eddy, the salesman, was looking desperate. He could see his commission evaporating away.

"The RAV4 is a great car", he suddenly stated, almost as an afterthought. "It's a 4-wheel drive, has a large rear compartment for a wheelchair and a high position for driver and passengers." I really had not thought for one moment of purchasing a 4-wheel drive vehicle but what Eddy had just said made sense. For starters, 4-wheel drive is safer in rain, ice and snow. The RAV4 has a truly fantastic commanding driving position. Assisting Dorothy into the front passenger seat was "easy-peasy". We ran the car about 10 miles and then back to the Toyota centre.

I was smiling as I applied the handbrake and withdrew the ignition key. "Wow", I said to myself, "I love you RAV4". Eddy watched as I turned Dorothy's legs through ninety degrees and helped her easily onto her feet.

I was pleased, Dorothy was pleased and Eddy was pleased. I had found the perfect car for someone with limited ability to manoeuvre in or out of a car. Dorothy had the pleasure of the RAV4 for eighteen months before her first stroke left her paralysed. Eight years after purchase, my RAV4 is the safest and best car I have ever owned.

Oh, by the way, it has a full-size spare wheel!

CHAPTER 33

THE MOVING FINGER WRITES AND WHO IS ERNIE?

The moving finger writes
And having writ, moves on
Nor all thy piety nor wit,
For half a second,
And it's gone.
Not the exact quote of Omar Khayyam

Dorothy already knew these famous lines by Omar Khayyam, years and years before she contracted Alzheimer's. She would quote them on numerous occasions. Then, of course, she understood the verse as a profundity, knowing its full meaning, that time can never be restored, once it has passed. But during the first stage of Alzheimer's and even into the second stage, Dorothy would repeat this small verse word for word.

And then along came ERNIE! I'm alluding to the machine which selects randomly the premium bond winning numbers - "Electronic Random Number Indicator Equipment". Prior to Alzheimer's, Dorothy had heard of ERNIE and knew that the machine selected the winning numbers but she didn't know the full title of the selection machine.

During the first stage, possibly in her third year of Alzheimer's, I taught her the full description title of ERNIE. It only took her about two days to fully learn it. Then every day she would say her Omar Khayyam, followed by ERNIE.

All good things come to an end. During the second stage I asked Dorothy one day to say her little party pieces. She could only repeat them with help from me. After   that she struggled with both for a couple of weeks or so before they had become a victim of Alzheimer's. Gone forever!!

CHAPTER 34

LET'S CALL ALZHEIMER'S SOMETHING ELSE

I was just playing around with ideas in my head this morning as I was having a cup of coffee in Dorothy's bedroom - that's the old sitting room as was.

Over a hundred years ago, people shunned the victims of cancer. It didn't really matter where the cancer was on a patient's anatomy, people thought that just by being in the vicinity of the cancer victim, it was contagious. Now people are better educated and understanding. Or are they? Neighbours have crossed the road, run into their houses or just "blanked" Dorothy and me. In over eight years, the local vicar, who lived next door, would neither visit Dorothy in hospital nor visit her at home. The neighbours on the other side of us complain about my tree overgrowing their property but never ask about or visit Dorothy.

The problem is that Alzheimer's is a disease of the brain. Do they think that it is contagious? No, I don't believe it's that. It's purely and simply something with which they cannot cope. Out of sight, out of mind? Yes, that's closer to the reality of how far too many people view Alzheimer's. It could happen to them? Of course it could but their "head in the sand" thinking is just as cancer was looked upon in the eighteen hundreds.

So, working on this theory, Alzheimer's will be an "O.K. disease" by 2150. We, the victims of Alzheimer's and their Carers can't wait that long. We're sick and tired of being ostracised and stigmatised because of their views that "head cases" should be in a "loony bin" or kept away from normal people!

Professor Alzheimer, the Austrian master surgeon of his era, whose name is synonymous with the title of our loved ones' illness, carried out many experiments on people who had died, not because of a brain disorder but a brain problem. He learned much about the malfunction of the human brain. But, of course, he didn't discover a cure. Now, over a hundred years later, there is still no cure for the disease which bears his name.

It is a great pity that Professor Alzheimer did not call the disease of the brain which he studied and researched during his life "cancer of the brain". If Dorothy's illness was cancer of the brain instead of Alzheimer's, I would have neighbours and ex-friends, queuing up to visit her!

That, dear reader, was the idea I had this morning whilst drinking a cup of coffee! Let's call Alzheimer's something else, let's just call it cancer!!!

CHAPTER 35

A FRIENDSHIP FOR ALL SEASONS

Celia and Chaz have been friends to Dorothy and me for over thirty years. Work colleagues of mine from way-back-when, our friendship has stood the test of time and of Alzheimer's.

When "so-called-friends" could not even cross the road or walk from next door to visit, or ask how Dorothy was keeping, these two stalwarts travelled a round trip of more than ninety miles to spend several hours with us. And I don't mean once or twice a year - more like every three weeks. Their cheerfulness, even though they had health issues of their own, helped to raise my spirits during Alzheimer's darkest days. Cee and Chaz reside in Freckleton, within easy reach of Lytham St. Annes. In the good old days, the four of us would meet up there and spend a happy day together.

The "Pig and Whistle" is a carvery (and pub) about six miles from Freckleton. Many are the occasions we've celebrated birthdays and just about any other reason to enjoy a fantastic meal together there, (We call it a "nosebag") at this popular rendezvous.

Dorothy, of course, hasn't made the journey to Freckleton for over seven years but true friends never let you down and Cee and Chaz are of that ilk.

I look forward to Cee's, Chaz's and my birthdays which the three of us still celebrate at the "Pig and Whistle". I'd be lying if I said that the occasions are not tinged with a degree of sadness but I know that Dorothy would wish it that we are able to enjoy ourselves in her absence.

When Dorothy and I were courting, I used to buy her a bag of Jamiesons's "Raspberry Ruffles" twice a week. Yes, Dorothy had a sweet tooth. I hadn't seen these chocolates for sale in decades.

I thought the firm had ceased trading. Imagine Dorothy's face when about ten years ago, Cee and Chaz found a sweet shop which stocked them and bought her a tin full of these delectable delights! They were rationed to her, five a day, but the tin lasted for a few weeks. Wow! What a lovely surprise for Dorothy! Thank you Cee and Chaz!

The friends that Dorothy and I still have show above all else: love, loyalty, sincerity, support and affection. Does this sound familiar to you dear reader? You deserve friends just like Cee and Chaz.

On this, the last day of 2012, I end this short chapter wishing Cee & Chaz and all our family and friends, Alzheimer's sufferers and their Carers throughout the world, a peaceful New Year - 2013.

CHAPTER 36

THE LAST VISIT TO BROADWAY SWIMMING BATHS

Many changes happened during Dorothy's second stage of Alzheimer's, especially towards the end of it and when she was no longer taking "Aricept".

The tandem skills had already gone but swimming was something she had done since being about six years old and she was a very good, strong swimmer. We were in the habit of visiting Broadway Swimming Baths every three or four weeks. We always went during a quiet period of the day and Dorothy loved the experience. Changing in a disabled cabin, we would make our way to the shallow end to walk down the steps and swim towards the deep end. I had stopped Dorothy from diving into the pool a year earlier, for obvious safety reasons. She enjoyed entering the water via the steps and when it reached her middle, off she went swimming to the deep end with me by her side.

Not so on this occasion!! I struck out towards the deep end but realised immediately that Dorothy was not alongside me. Glancing round I saw that she was not swimming, just standing there. Joining her, I went through the breaststroke sequence with her, fully expecting swimming to commence. No!! I tried several times, even taking Dorothy's weight under my arm and walking slowly. Definitely no sign that she had ever swam in her life.

Dave, the lifeguard, spotted that Dorothy was not swimming as she normally did. He was aware that Dorothy had Alzheimer's. Five minutes later, Dave passed to me buoyancy aids to fit around Dorothy's waist, neck, wrists and ankles. She was floating with the help of these aids but without making strokes, swimming was impossible.

138

For the next 20 minutes with Dave giving Dorothy all the verbal encouragement he could, I was unable to assist her to swim. Another door had been slammed in Dorothy's face. All those previous occasions, spread over many years, she had swam with Alzheimer's - now that skill had succumbed to the illness.

I thanked Dave for his help, dried and dressed Dorothy before leaving Broadway Pool for the very last time.

So sad, so very sad, but Alzheimer's always has the last word. Dancing, cycling and now swimming gone! All gone!

I could feel the tears behind my eyes as we walked towards the car. "Never mind, Sweetheart", I said, "I'll make you a lovely cup of tea instead".

CHAPTER 37

A SURPRISE BIRTHDAY PRESENT

Dorothy's birthday was fast approaching in 1996. I had no idea at all what to buy for her, so decided to drop her off at the Carisbrooke Centre and have a look around the shops in the centre of Manchester.

Walking along fashionable Deansgate, I found myself window-shopping outside a sports shop. Looking at the various items for sale, I suddenly saw a gleaming set of bowls, complete with a leather bag, in which to store them (and transport them around, of course).

Next minute, I was inside the shop and an assistant was showing me bowls, for use on Crown Green bowing greens. It hadn't occurred to me until then but as I had said that I'd take a set, ladies weight, I realised that I'd need a second set for myself and a bright yellow "Jack".

Dorothy and I had played bowls at Heaton Park on many occasions in the past, but, just starting her third year with Alzheimer's, I wondered if she could still play. I need not have concerned myself: on her birthday, a few days later, she could hardly wait to jump in the car and try out her birthday gift from me.

The afternoon of 28 May 1996 was perfect for bowling. I explained the principle of the "bias", which turns the bowl to the left or the right before homing in on the "Jack". Dorothy hadn't forgotten how to play and I recall thinking to myself, as play progressed, "Here's Dorothy, three years into Alzheimer's, playing bowls as though all is well".

We bowled for several years after 1996 but one day Dorothy forgot everything about bowls and she started to throw the bowls in all directions. A little later her tandem skills were forgotten and swimming also became a thing of the past. We still had that lovely walk around Hollingworth Lake left but eventually the walk was done with Dorothy in her wheelchair.

I would gladly return, right now, to Dorothy's wheelchair days. Alzheimer's is cruel, all the way to the end!

Make the most dear Carer, whilst your loved one still has any of their basic skills to participate in any kind of sporty recreation, or just plain walking, together. Once your love one's mobility has gone forever, only wheelchair walks are left to you.

I hope this chapter may have given you the idea of bowling. If you don't own bowls but you live quite close to "Horner Towers", drop in for a "cuppa" and borrow ours for a few days. You would be very welcome!

CHAPTER 38

A DAY OUT AT THE SEASIDE

Dorothy and I made the most of that invaluable period of time from the diagnosis of Alzheimer's right up to her first stroke. Bear in mind, that Stage 1 is barely discernible from the norm, except our loved ones require total supervision. In stage 2 the Alzheimer's is quite obvious, even to passers-by, but getting about should not be too much of a problem.

This chapter recalls a typical Sunday trip to Lytham St. Annes, quite close to the world-famous Blackpool but a much prettier and much quieter place. Blackpool caters more for young families and teenagers, whereas Lytham St. Annes is more for the older generations.

After an adequate breakfast, I would prepare our packed lunch. Dorothy loved salad on her teacakes or muffins, so mixed salad teacakes it would be. I would have purchased a half dozen pack of "Mr. Kipling's" (exceedingly good) apple pies and a shiny apple to finish off. A flask of boiling hot coffee would complete the picnic hamper.

The trip to London only requires driving along the M62 and the M1. By contrast the journey to Lytham St. Annes, one-fifth the distance, takes in the M60, M62, M61, M6 and M55. Consequently, the journey can be completed in an hour.

Parking is plentiful in Lytham St. Annes. We normally parked on the main road adjacent to a picnic bench, set back a few feet from the pavement. This enables day trippers to face the beach and sea, or, alternatively, face the pavement, "people watch" and just let the world go by.

Dorothy would be mega excited. She knew that Lytham St. Annes was much different from the dusty pavements of

Manchester. Besides, "Horner Towers" can become increasingly "samey" without at least one trip out somewhere each week.

Watching out for Eddie Stobart lorries, we would thread our way from one motorway to the next. Before very long, I would be parking by "our" picnic bench and at around 10.00 a.m. our day out was truly underway!

Dorothy and I have always enjoyed walking. The day would be comprised, in the main, of two very long walks, sightseeing as we ambled along. The morning walk would take us until nearly 1.00 p.m. Lunch on the picnic bench, followed an hour later by our walk in the opposite direction. I estimate that in the day we would walk about eight miles.

The morning walk was punctuated by several stops. Dorothy loved window-shopping. If the shop was open we would have a browse and maybe purchase something. W.H. Smith was always worthwhile to look round. But the shop Dorothy looked forward to the most was Woolworths. Like to guess why? The "pick and mix", of course! She would deliberate for fully five minutes, selecting "one of these and two of those". Eventually, happy with her selection, off we went to the till to have them weighed. I rationed the sweets out to her. Otherwise all of them would be eaten in a very short time. Also, with all the sweets consumed, the picnic would be less appetising. "We'll save half for the afternoon, Sweetheart", I would say.

For years Dorothy and I had planned on retiring to Lytham St. Annes. We looked at the "For Sale" properties as they came into view and would appraise them (or not) and discuss how much we thought the asking price would be.

A popular estate agent at that time was Janet Dunderdale. An unusual surname for sure. Dorothy would repeat the name over and over again, accompanied with peals of laughter. No disrespect Ms. Dunderdale but you brought laughter into the world of an Alzheimer victim. Thank you.

We would cross the road to join the end of the promenade. A steep slope led to the beach. I had shown Dorothy how, with short steps, she could negotiate the slope safely.

Now the beach. The best part of the morning! Razor shells lay around in large quantities, the result of the seagulls constant search for food. Dorothy loved stamping on the delicate shells remains, reducing them to a thousand fragments. How she enjoyed this childish play! The look of joy on her face was fascinating to see. There was something quite compulsive in the destruction of these delicate shells. The "ker-crunch", followed by a slight popping noise could be described as relaxing even. All I really know is that Dorothy enjoyed this innocent destruction and as we all know, laughter is wonderful medicine.

Almost back to the car. I could see that the picnic bench was unoccupied and Dorothy had noticed this too. She would almost run the last hundred yards to ensure the bench was "ours". I would bring the picnic hamper from the car and spread out the wholesome food between us. "Help yourself Dorothy" I would whisper, pointing to the salad teacakes. She always enjoyed her food but the sea air makes a healthy appetite even healthier. Finishing the picnic with a cup of coffee was perfect.

The afternoon walk was in the opposite direction. Again, properties for sale would catch our eye. Some were as large as mansions but Dorothy enjoyed appraising them. The "White Church" is a local landmark. It took its name from its exterior being finished entirely in white: marble or tile. We headed towards this landmark, its size increasing with every step. Dorothy, even with Alzheimer's, would bid everyone coming towards us a "Good afternoon". She looked the picture of health to all and sundry, but she could not have found her own way back to the car, not for a thousand pounds.

In the earlier days of Alzheimer's we would walk beyond the "White Church" until we arrived at a windmill. It's in a wonderful state of preservation and it looks as though it is a family home.

Time to set off back to the car and a hot coffee before returning home. The "pick and mix" were now history! "Keep your eyes open for Eddie Stobarts" I would say and Dorothy's eyes would light up in a smile.

Four Eddie Stobart lorries later, yes they must work the Sunday shift, and after just over an hour of motorway we were parking up outside "Horner Towers". Two eggs and a plateful of golden chips was still Dorothy's favourite meal after a day out. She would stand and watch me as I peeled the potatoes and cooked the food.

There can be happy days during Alzheimer's. You have just read all about a very happy day in the life of an Alzheimer's victim and her Carer!

CHAPTER 39

THE TAJ MAHAL IN ALL ITS GLORY, FOLLOWED BY AN INDIAN TUMMY BUG

Yes, dear readers, that's the order of play for this chapter. The almost beyond-belief experience of witnessing sunrise striking the Taj Mahal, followed by the incredibly horrible experience of "Montezuma's revenge". Ugh!

We had already spent a couple of weeks in Goa. The fascinating sub-continent is unique: unlike any other coastal resort we had already visited.

The hotel staff and all the local people had only one thing on their minds as far as tourists were concerned - to make their stay a memorable one! We were only bed and breakfast at "Whispering Palms"; our other meals we ate mainly in the village. Even the name of the hotel conjures up a picture of swaying palm trees and splendid ocean views.

Dorothy and I had pre-booked four days in New Delhi, two of the days to be spent in Agra; the main reason for that destination being the "Taj Mahal". From the coast of Goa on the Indian Ocean to New Delhi in the far north of India, almost as far as the Himalayas, Tibet and Kashmir, is a mighty distance but the 747 made light work of it and we looked forward to seeing so many interesting sights. Immediately on landing we were transferred to a decrepit looking coach which I'm sure would have failed its MOT in Britain.

We were to spend two days in Agra, followed by two days in New Delhi.

There is no airport at Agra and anyone wishing to see the Taj Mahal has to endure a six-hours coach journey along the most mountainous, narrow, badly repaired roads I had ever seen. Agra is due south of New Delhi, so off we set. I now know what all the little animals and rabbits' feet were doing situated on the dash board, and swinging from the windscreen. Lucky charms!

At first I thought our coach was in a race but our driver assured us that he always drove that way. "You want to get there, don't you?" he shouted laughingly when asked to slow down. "Could be a play on words there", I said to Dorothy. Every mode of transport, including horse and carts, used this, the only road out of New Delhi to Agra. Overtaking a horse and cart is a tricky manoeuvre due to the on-coming traffic. I shut my eyes on two or three occasions but the lucky charms were doing their stuff.

"Look down there, into the valley", chortled our budding F1 driver. We all looked. "Cars, lorries and coaches, when they leave the road, are left there - too expensive to bring them back up". We nodded, along with the lucky, nodding black cat sitting on the dash board and I wondered how many of his nine lives were left. On arrival outside our hotel in Agra, Michael Schumacher's Indian half cousin informed us that he had knocked more than ten minutes off his previous New Delhi to Agra record. I thought that he may have knocked one or two years off our lives.

The concierge at the hotel took our requirements for breakfast the following morning. "We advise an early night, a maid will waken you at 4.30 a.m." No problem then.

Our breakfast was ready for 5.00 a.m. and the coach left at 5.30 a.m. Only a few minutes drive to the world-famous Taj Mahal.

Oh! I almost forgot to mention that Dorothy and I had an omelette for our breakfast. Something safe and simple for such an early meal.

At the Taj Mahal car/coach park, our driver had taken our money to purchase entrance tickets. He advised us to employ a guide to show us around, one guide to two visitors. He would take photographs and explain everything about the site and the mausoleum, which the Taj Mahal is. "Back here for 10.45 a.m.", he said. "Enjoy the best sights in all of India."

147

The sun was within minutes of striking the Taj Mahal, which already looked majestic in the half-light. We had employed our guide for three hours and in perfect English he was explaining where to take our initial photographs from. He was also taking snaps of Dorothy and me. We later had the opportunity to buy as many snaps as we required, when he called at the hotel the following morning.

Suddenly, the sun's rays hit the marble miracle that is the Taj Mahal. Dorothy and I both agreed that it was a fantastic experience and that it should be one of the seven wonders of the world.

I won't write here how truly remarkable those few hours were, if you, dear reader, have already visited the Taj Mahal, you will already know. If you haven't, then try and rectify that omission, if possible, sometime in the future.

Back in the 1950s coach, the driver informed us that we were on our way to visit a magnificent fort, hundreds of years old. Dorothy and I relaxed in our seats, quite tired by our early start that morning and the excitement of the wonders of the last few hours. Suddenly, Dorothy leaned forward in her seat and said "Feel sick, going to be sick". A thought struck me: yesterday during that appalling journey of hours from New Delhi, she hadn't felt sick and now on a slow journey, most sedate even, she did feel sick.

I asked the driver, "How far to the fort please?" "About 3 minutes", he replied but I knew Dorothy could not wait even one minute. Desperately I looked around for a sick bag. None, I didn't even have a handkerchief in my pocket. Before I could tell Dorothy to be sick on the floor of the coach and not on the couple in the seats in front of us, something happened which I shall never forget. Bear in mind, that Dorothy had Alzheimer's, albeit in the second/middle stage, but she then did something that I had not thought to do. The split second before she vomited Dorothy grabbed her linen sunhat from her head and used it as a receptacle. "Well done, Sweetheart", I muttered.

148

I placed the hat in a couple of plastic bags which the driver gave me and put it in the coach's storage compartment. Later, back at the hotel, I would wash the hat in shampoo and conditioner to restore it to pristine condition (Really worked too!)

The guide showing our party of two coach loads around, was the biggest Indian gentleman I had ever seen. Very tall, at say 6 ft 7 ins, he must have weighed in at well over 30 stones. He knew this fort as though it were his home and he made the tour of it very interesting. Starting from the ground level we made our way up to the very top, the battlements. From this lofty height I could see the Taj Mahal in the far distance. I pointed this fact out to Dorothy who immediately blurted out, "Toilet, toilet please". I said to her that the tour was almost over and we would find the toilets then. Almost as soon as I had said those few words, I realised that I too needed the toilets. Very, very soon, the sooner the better!

I approached the tour guide and asked him where the toilets were. "None in the fort" he replied. "I'll show you in ten minutes when I've finished off this level". I looked at Dorothy. At this stage of her Alzheimer's she wasn't incontinent but if she felt like I did, she couldn't delay for very long. Taking the law into my own hands, I addressed the whole tour party and said that I was sorry but the guide was leaving them for a few minutes whilst he showed us where the toilets were. I quickly realised that the Indian guide was "knock-kneed" and very unfit. "Can we run?" I implored him. He couldn't! On the first level I knew the Indian guide was almost exhausted. He pointed to a long slope leading to the street outside. "Down the slope", he gasped. He couldn't move another inch!

Dorothy and I ran down the slope, almost running into a mother pushing a pram. "Toilets please", I pleaded. The young mother just pointed across the road to her left. With my thanks almost carried away in the breeze, I took Dorothy's hand. As we dodged between the traffic, I could see and smell the toilets. A truly Eureka moment!!

149

I would gladly have paid five pounds each for the use of the two holes in the floor we used. With hardly a second to spare, I must add.

A few minutes later I paid the attendant ten rupees each and off we went to meet up with the rest of the party.

It wouldn't have taken Sherlock Holmes a minute to work out what had happened since breakfast time. Our omelettes were obviously infected by using impure water. Only Dorothy and I had an omelette for breakfast - lucky for the others, unlucky for us.

The rest of the visit to Agra went very well. We didn't finish upside down in the valley on the way back to New Delhi, where we enjoyed a couple of days sight-seeing.

Whenever anyone talks about Agra I listen and at the end, say with a laugh, "But did you have to sprint for the local toilets outside the fort's entrance?"

Do you know something? I wouldn't have missed it for the world!

CHAPTER 40

AS A CARER, DO I REALLY
EXPECT TOO MUCH?

As the days blend seamlessly into each other and become weeks, months and years, we, dear Carers, rely more and more on our family, friends and neighbours. We welcome a visit, a telephone call or maybe just a wave and a smile from that near neighbour from around the corner.

"No man is an island" wrote John Donne in the 17th Century but just as true today as in yesteryear. Perhaps your loved one will become like Dorothy? She hasn't spoken a single word in years but, where visits are concerned, our family and friends become increasingly important but have busy lives and could live many miles away. Consequently, home visits are really special and much appreciated.

A family acquaintance called to deliver his Christmas card on Christmas Eve. He is in the age generation below mine and of high intellect, being a "man of letters". He asked me if many neighbours or local friends would call to wish Dorothy and me the "Compliments of the Season". I replied that it would be highly unlikely, going off the experience of previous Christmases. I went on to add that our erstwhile friends and neighbours in the area, were conspicuous by their absence. I stated that Dorothy and I would have visited *them* in a roles-reversal scenario. I added that their stigmatising of Dorothy and myself over the years showed a lack of any respect and also that I thought that they *should* have visited us. Imagine my absolute surprise when this family acquaintance looked me straight in the eye and said, You shouldn't expect anyone to come here and visit. In fact, it's wrong of you to even think it".

So, where has the "milk of human kindness" disappeared to? What could I say in defence of his concept of our situation, which

151

would make him see that my expectations should be more realistic?

Prince Charles has asked nursing staff in hospitals and nursing homes to show more compassion during the performance of their duties. He shouldn't *need* to ask for this. It should be a prerequisite in any nursing post, but lack of compassion is now the downside in too many hospitals. Mid-Staffordshire Hospital is a case in point where, due to poor nursing practices, 1,200 patients died in just four years.

I know we live in austere, increasingly violent times but the period I recall of the Second World War and the aftermath of rationing and deprivation, seems somewhat better than how society has shaped our modern world since.

So, unaware as she is, Dorothy has lived through another Christmas. During the period three months ago, when she had pneumonia, it seemed very unlikely that she would.

I live in hope for 2013 and wish you all, dear readers, "A Happy New Year".

CHAPTER 41

SOME INTERESTING FACTS ABOUT ALZHEIMER'S AND DEMENTIA

Alzheimer's is a global problem, Its progression is unrelenting and, in reality, is terrible and shocking for the victim, the Carer and the connected family.

I would die a happy man if, during my remaining years (I will be 75 years old in April), a magical cure could be found. Too late for Dorothy but Alzheimer's will stretch way, way into the future and there's a lot of misery in store for millions of people worldwide.

Alzheimer's is easily diagnosed by a CT scan. Hence, younger victims have been diagnosed and are referred to as having Alzheimer's. Older people - the over seventies - are considered to have Dementia or Senile Dementia and are unlikely to have had a CT scan.

The information which follows refers to the United Kingdom but European and world figures are of a similar percentage and figures will be more, or less, depending on populations.

The number of people with Alzheimer's/Dementia In the United Kingdom has been estimated from the known populations in 2005:

England: 575,000
Northern Ireland: 16,000
Scotland: 56,000
Wales: 37,000

Total number of Alzheimer's/Dementia sufferers in the United Kingdom: 684,000 (Approx).

Divided into age groups:
40 - 64 years:1 in 1,400
65 - 69 years:1 in 100
70 - 79 years :1 in 25
80 - 95 years:1 in 6
95+ years:1 in 3

Not officially known are the numbers of Alzheimer's victims below the age of 40. Some are in the 20-30 years age group even!

It is thought that by 2021, 940,000 people in the United Kingdom will be affected by Alzheimer's/Dementia. This figure could rise to 1,700,000 by 2051. One in 14 people over 65 years of age, and 1 in 6 people over 80 years of age, could have one form or another of Dementia.

Alzheimer's is the most common form of Dementia. The proportion is assessed as follows:
Alzheimer's disease (AD):62%
Vascular dementia (VaD:17%
Mixed dementia (AD & VaD):10%
Dementia with Lewy bodies: 4%
Fronto-temporal dementia: 2%
Parkinson's dementia: 2%
Other dementias: 3%
Alzheimer's is fairly rare among people under 65. The figure for the 20 - 54 age group is approximately 15,000 but 20 -64 rises to approximately 46,000. Bear in mind these two sets of figures include population figures which include children and persons in the up to twenty years of age group. The majority of dementia

154

sufferers are in the age group 65 - 95+. The odds of someone contracting Alzheimer's in the 20 - 54 age group are 1 in 4,350!

Two-thirds of people with dementia are female.

The proportion of people with dementia doubles for every 5-year age group.

One- third of all people over 95 have dementia.

Family Carers for people with Alzheimer's/Dementia save the United Kingdom £6 billion per year.

Two-thirds of people with Alzheimer's/Dementia live in their own home or the Carer's home. Only one-third live in a care home attended by professionals.

Only 2% of medical research funding is allocated to Alzheimer's: for every £300 spent each year on research for Alzheimer's and Cancer combined, £11 is allocated for each Alzheimer's patient; £289 for each Cancer patient.

Every 71 seconds someone in the United Kingdom develops Alzheimer's.

There are over 5 million people in Europe with Alzheimer's/Dementia. This is the same number of sufferers as there are in the United States. There are at least 24 million people with Alzheimer's/Dementia throughout the world: by 2025 this number could rise to 34 million.

No one knows what causes Alzheimer's. There is, as yet, no known cure for it.

Alzheimer's Society (UK, except Scotland)
Devon House
58 St. Katharine's Way
London E1W 1LB
Tel. No. 020 7423 3500
Helpline: 0300 222 1122
email: enquiries@Alzheimers.org.uk
Web: www.Alzheimers.org.uk

Alzheimer's Scotland - Action on Dementia
Tel: 0131 243 1453
Helpline: 0808 808 3000
email: Alzheimers@alzscot.org
Web: www.alzscot.org

CHAPTER 42

"OFF TO LIVE ON THE KENT COAST"

If Dorothy had not contracted Alzheimer's, we would have left Manchester round about the time of our retirement, circa 1998. Both Mancunians by birth and domicile, we had talked of a little "bolt hole" abroad, and a permanent home on the coast, a complete change of scenery in which to enjoy our retirement.

However, perhaps making plans too far ahead is a little bit arrogant, because none of us knows for sure what the future has in store for us. So, the retirement we are all hoping for is a complete lottery. No different for Dorothy and me than it is for anyone else. I've never suffered from self-pity ever, so like many millions of people throughout the world, when things go "pear-shaped", we all have to accept it.

During the summer of 2005 my daughter Liz and her husband Francis, invited Dorothy and me to spend a week with them and our grandson, Alex, at a little resort on the Kent coast called St. Margaret's-at-Cliffe. Little did I know that this holiday was to be the last ever that Dorothy and I would spend together before her stroke in 2006.

The week we spent in St. Margaret's-at-Cliffe was wonderful. Great company, drives around Kent and fabulous walks along the promenades of lovely Kentish seaside resorts. Dorothy could only walk a few steps at this stage of her Alzheimer's but I pushed her all over the place; Dover, Canterbury, Deal, Sandwich, Herne Bay, Broadstairs and Tankerton.

I remember Dover especially well. The castle there is majestic and the harbour with ferries to and from the Continent arriving and leaving constantly. Very interesting.

On a sour note, I left our car in a disabled parking bay. Dorothy's disabled badges had expired two days previously and I had added a printed card on the dashboard next to the badges stating, "New badges in the post". The "jobs worth" traffic warden, even though she saw me arrive back at my car, pushing Dorothy in her wheelchair, said she would give me a fixed penalty fine, if I didn't move the car within the next five minutes. Nice!!

The following day I fell in love with a tiny seaside resort called Tankerton. It lies between Whitstable and Herne Bay and only 8 miles from Canterbury. I'd never even heard of a place called Tankerton, until that day. I had visions of, sometime in the future, pushing Dorothy's wheelchair along the promenade, then resting on a bench and looking out to sea. Perfect!

Things moved on rapidly towards the latter part of 2005. Liz, my elder daughter, placed my name on the mailing lists of several estate agents in the Tankerton area and I placed "Horner Towers" in the hands of an auction company.

Not a very good company to be quite honest with you. The auctioneer came to assess "Horner Towers" for the purpose of its inclusion in his next auction catalogue. How anyone can miscount the reception rooms in a house is beyond me. There are three receptions rooms, have been since 1933, and yet, in the catalogue the property was described as having two reception rooms.

Another point of interest. At that time, two windows on the gable end were not UVPC double glazed. In the catalogue the description read, "partly double glazed". He said I was "splitting hairs" Mmm. Off to a bad start you could say, dear reader. Needless to say, the bidding did not reach the reserve price. And that was that.

I sold "Horner Towers" to a lovely couple called Jean and Chris. They followed me out of the auction room having inspected the house a few days previously. We agreed on a price there and then and shook hands on the deal.

A brand-new bungalow, just off the promenade at Tankerton was my target, and the builder accepted my very-near-offer. Everything in the garden was looking rosy.

Until ....

On Wednesday, 8 February 2006, Dorothy had her massive first stroke. (As described in Chapter 21). She was to remain in North Manchester General Hospital for many weeks.

I, of course, informed Jean and Chris of the situation. They and their family had set their hearts on moving to New Moston. Needing to be 100% honest with these lovely, thoroughly decent people, I told them that if Dorothy did not live through the stroke and the following weeks, then I would go through with the house sale.

With the greatest reluctance, after nearly three months in hospital, with Dorothy's health issues precarious, I had to break the news to them that the house sale was off. The 320 miles journey to Tankerton would have killed Dorothy. I had no other option. It is one of the hardest, most cruel decisions I have ever had to make in all my life.

Jean and Chris kept in touch for almost twelve months but, eventually, the telephone calls and visits stopped and I presume they found an alternative house.

I still received the Auctioneer's and Solicitor's bills for their fees. An invoice for nearly £1,800 for the move that didn't happen.

Sorry, Jean and Chris, maybe sometime in the future, you'll end up at "Horner Towers".

CHAPTER 43

OUR THANKS TO THE COMMUNITY CARE WORKERS, DISTRICT NURSES AND DIETICIANS

Dorothy was discharged from North Manchester General Hospital mid-May 2006. She was paralysed from the neck downwards, her arms constantly set with her hands level with her collarbones. There was movement in her hands and she could reach her mouth with her fingers and thumb but only her right hand could reach her mouth. I'm supposing that if Dorothy had been left-handed, then she would have sucked the fingers and thumb on her left hand.

How she enjoys this baby-like habit! I need to supervise this at all times to ensure that her fingers or thumb do not cause Dorothy to start to choke.

For the first six months after being installed in a hospital bed in the sitting room at "Horner Towers", Dorothy had all her needs attended to by "yours truly".

This routine embraced the whole twenty-four hours of each day, commencing around 7.30 a.m. with a bed-bath and a clean nightie change. Bed linen would be changed weekly or when wet, caused by an ill-fitting pad or the pad exceeding saturation point. Feeding Dorothy was time consuming, each of the three meals taking approximately one hour each, due to slow chewing and hesitant swallowing.

After six months of these assorted carer's duties, I was absolutely worn out! There is no section of the NHS which provides a homecare service. Consequently, private companies, in addition to care homes and nursing homes, assist in your home, administering all types of care from just making someone's breakfast or tea, dressing a patient (client), purchasing the weekly shop, as well as more intensive care of the type I was providing for Dorothy.

Now an assortment of trained care workers, seven days a week, three times a day, give Dorothy the attention she requires. That consists of a one-hour morning call and two half-hour calls, one at mid-day and the other at 7.00 p.m. I administer the medication at 11.00 p.m., prior to the last pad change of the day.

I wish to express my gratitude to the scores of ladies who, during the last six-and-a-half years, have taken a whole load of weight from my working/caring day. Thank you so much! Very much appreciated!

The most regular callers at the time of writing my book being Jean, Sue, Lou, Elaine and Vicky. I thank each and every lady who has ever called at "Horner Towers" and cared for Dorothy!

I would also like to thank the NHS district nurses: Anne, the two Julies and John.

Also deserving of my thanks are the dieticians and the Nutricia staff, who call to make sure that Dorothy's PEG system is always operating correctly. Thank you so much!

A true cynic would say, "Why thank a person for doing the job they are paid to do?" I thank Dorothy's caring staff by word-of-mouth each time they exit my front door for their services and now I have thanked them, in print.

The day that we, as a society, stop thanking each other for whatever we do will be living proof that, as a people, we have not moved very far from the mouth of the cave!

EPILOGUE

I well remember starting this short book on 1 October 2011, fifteen months ago. It has, indeed, been a journey of 1,000 miles. Perhaps the journey is nowhere near over? I need to find a publisher prepared to take a chance on this, the only book I will ever write.

That Dorothy would still be alive fifteen months after writing the first line of the Preface, is perhaps a minor miracle in itself.

In March I shall start on the twentieth year of my duties as a Carer. You will have read of the trials and tribulations of a Carer and his loved-one. Those years have really been a labour of love.

With my half-full glass, I have seen all three stages of this catastrophic disease, giving to Dorothy the love which started on 5 December 1955, and which has matured, grown and inspired me to superhuman dedication, allied to the patience, without which a Carer cannot even half function, every new situation has been made possible to endure and respond to.

Alzheimer's is unlike cancer or any other wasting disease. With cancer, a victim will engage in conversation and recognise loved ones right to the very end. It will devastate the body but the brain remains intact. With Alzheimer's the very last traces of who he/she was, are destroyed. Nothing is left at the end, nothing inside or outside of the person we knew and loved.

As we watch this slow disintegration of our loved one, the sadness is unique. Indescribable in its intensity. In an unguarded moment, I can walk into Dorothy's bedroom and, on seeing her, start to weep. That unguarded moment releases feelings so intense that I need to keep them under "lock and key" for most of the time.

The realisation of the retirement we never had, grandchildren she never knew, golden memories now forgotten, everyday routines and life experiences gone forever because Alzheimer's has decreed that the brain must deteriorate until it ceases to exist.

Do not think, dear Carer, that your loved one is better off in a nursing home. You may think you are at the end of your tether and that your patience has finally snapped. If I can do this caring, right until the very end, then so can you. Be assertive to the demands of Alzheimer's! Remember, one day at a time. Your loved one will live longer in your care because the nursing home cannot give him/her the love and devotion you give on a daily basis.

On 26 December 1955, Dorothy and I watched a movie called, "Love is a Many Splendoured Thing". Dorothy's favourite lines from this, her all time favourite film, are:

"We have not missed, you and I,
We have not missed,
That many splendoured thing."

I knew that our love for each other was inspirational, I could feel that from the very first day. Love is the most precious thing in all our lives. It is so priceless!

Without Dorothy, my life would always have been empty. Anything and everything good that has happened in my life, happened because of her.

My very best wishes to you all.

J.M. Horner (Carer)